THOMAS BEWICK

My Life

Thomas Bewick as a young man.
Painting by George Gray. *Laing Gallery*

THOMAS BEWICK
My Life

EDITED AND WITH AN INTRODUCTION BY
IAIN BAIN
WITH NUMEROUS WOOD-ENGRAVINGS
AND WATERCOLOURS BY THE
AUTHOR

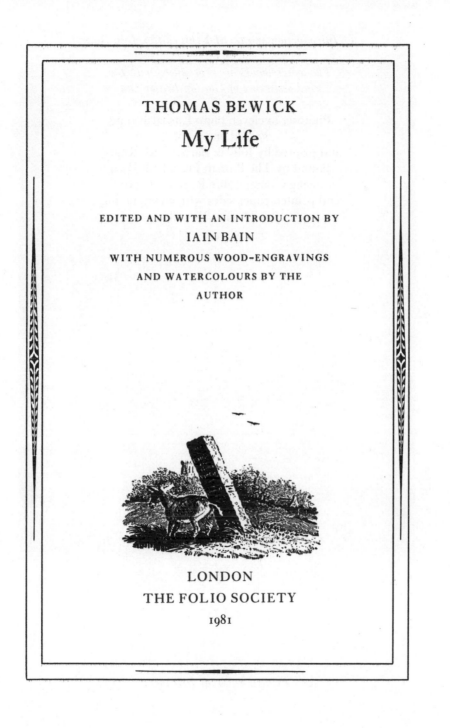

LONDON
THE FOLIO SOCIETY
1981

Photoset in eleven point Ehrhardt type
spaced one point
and printed by Jolly & Barber Ltd, Rugby
bound by The Pitman Press Ltd, Bath
using Grange Fibre Regency Cloth
and printed paper sides with an engraving
by Thomas Bewick

Printed in Great Britain

CONTENTS

[5]

COLOUR PLATES

Original size reproductions of 31 watercolour drawings for the *British Birds*, 1797 and 1804 can be found facing pages 32, 33, 48, 49, 96, 97, 112, 113, 128, 129, 144, 145, 160, 161, 176 and 177.

⫸ NOTE ⫷
ON THE ILLUSTRATIONS

The first edition of the *Memoir* was decorated with a selection of engravings originally intended for Bewick's unpublished *History of British Fishes*. For the most part these have here been replaced by sixty-seven of his best subjects for the *British Birds*, the *History of Quadrupeds* and the *Fables of Aesop*. All are shown in their original size. The figures of animals and birds are all Bewick's work, but a number of the tail-piece vignettes in the *British Birds* were engraved by his talented apprentice Luke Clennell: some of these can be found on pages 44, 84, 88, 90, 120, 153 and 159. Two designs by Bewick for the *Fables of Aesop*, cut by apprentices under his supervision, can be found on pages 70 and 99. The colour reproductions of the preliminary drawings, also shown in their original size, have been taken from my own two-volume *Watercolours and Drawings of Thomas Bewick and his Workshop Apprentices*, Gordon Fraser, 1981. The birds were all drawn by Bewick; the tail-piece vignettes were finished by Robert Johnson, his apprentice between 1786 and 1794 (see pp. 181–85); in general Bewick provided the preliminary idea in pencil and then gave Johnson the task of working them up into finished colour drawings for transfer to the wood block. A close comparison of the landscape backgrounds to the birds with those in the tail-pieces will soon make apparent the greater degree of finish employed by Johnson. Many of the drawings display the tell-tale crease marks made when the paper was folded over the wood block during the transfer process which has already been described in the Introduction. The drawing of the Goose facing page 96 is shown beside its related engraving. Many of the tail-pieces have a strong narrative content which is fully discussed in my own *Thomas Bewick Vignettes*, Scolar Press, 1978. Bewick's engravings are notoriously difficult to reproduce owing to his technique of lowering the surface of the block. All the engravings in this edition have been reproduced from the Memorial Edition of Bewick's Works 1885–7, generally acknowledged as the best printed source.

Grateful thanks are due to the Natural History Society of Northumbria [NHSN] and the Trustees of the British Museum [BM] for permission to reproduce drawings in their collection, and to Gordon Fraser Limited for permission to use their colour originals. Two of the drawings are from the editor's collection.

INTRODUCTION

Celebrated as a wood engraver, and in his time a crucial influence on the vigorous growth of a popular interest in natural history, Thomas Bewick has continued to hold the world's regard to the present day. No history of the relief print can be written without reference to him, and his engravings of animals and birds and scenes of the Northumberland countryside continue to delight succeeding generations. Not a year passes without his work being reproduced for uses of every kind – from the labelling of fertilizer sacks and bread wrappers to the decoration of writing paper, pottery and books. His work has indeed become better known than his name.

In 1822, six years before he died, Bewick set himself to write a memoir of his life, prompted by his family and spurred on by the threatened attempts of several contemporaries whom he felt to be in no proper position to do so themselves. He began by addressing himself to his children, through his daughter Jane, but as he proceeded and thoughts of posterity began to loom, the personal voice developed a more public tone. He would have been surprised, though not ungratified to discover his memoir a minor classic, but such it has become – not only on account of his importance as an artist-engraver without equal of his kind, but also for what he made of a unique record of a north-country childhood and life as a craftsman in late Georgian England. It was his natural and early developed gift for a penetrating clarity of observation, his 'painter's eye', that was to give the book its lasting qualities, qualities which overcame an undeniable unevenness in its construction.

Born in 1753, the son of the tenant of a small eight-acre farm and an adjacent colliery, Bewick has too often been looked upon as an unlettered peasant genius, but as with Burns – whose poetry he so much admired and with whom Ruskin was to compare him – this simple romantic view of him cannot be supported by the facts. His *Memoir*, and his correspondence which survives in considerable quantity, show him to have been vigorously articulate. His account of his father gives a hint of how he came to be so.

It is the early part of the *Memoir*, which tells of the time of his boyhood on the banks of the river Tyne, that has inspired the greatest affection for the book. His intensely felt recollection of Northumberland in winter cold and summer breeze, of pranks on the river, of the cruelty of huntsmen and the pleasures of angling, has a serenity and sensitivity reminiscent of Wordsworth's *Prelude*. As he so vividly remembers, it was during this time that his compulsion to draw became so firmly fixed. These first fourteen years were to have a lasting influence on his work as an artist and engraver, and his love of the countryside and its inhabitants was to be a constant source of refreshment to him in the later years of long application to his closely confined life at the workbench. Living was not easy for the family of eight children, of which he was the eldest, and his independent waywardness as a child brought him severe restraint and discipline. This and his strict schooling under the village parson was largely to account for his later and sometimes forbiddingly moralistic outlook on life.

When Bewick was fourteen, his godmother's friendship with the talented Beilby family – artists, engravers and glass enamellers in Newcastle – brought him to a most fortunate apprenticeship with Ralph Beilby who at that time had established the only general engraving business in the town. The then rapid growth of Newcastle's prosperity, founded on the coal trade and the industries it supported, provided a source for a very great variety of work. The contacts Bewick made with the shop's extraordinarily diverse customers, many of them men of talent and learning, were to bring him lasting benefit throughout his life. His master's self-sufficiency, his willingness to take on every class of work and to adapt his tools whenever necessary, was taken up readily by the pupil. Beilby was like Gregson, the parson schoolmaster, a disciplinarian, and Bewick was given little opportunity for idle pleasures. From what can be discovered in the family papers, his relationship with the Beilbys was not an easy one, for they appear to have condescended to the country-boy apprentice, and this condescension, especially that of Ralph's wife, the daughter of a Newcastle watchmaker, rankled with Bewick and his family to the end of his life.

The business records show that the amount of wood engraving that passed through the workshop was very small indeed when compared with its general trade in metal engraving. Nevertheless, Bewick's sympathy for the medium and his early success with it won him a premium from the Society for the Encouragement of Arts. It was awarded for some of the book illustrations he engraved towards the end of his apprenticeship and it set the seal on his future reputation.

After the statutory seven years Bewick left his master and then continued to work at home for the local printers and publishers, until the early summer of 1776 when he took himself off on a five-hundred mile walk from Newcastle through the Highlands of Scotland – he was a formidable pedestrian and continued to be so. This was an interlude that produced one of the most delightful passages in the *Memoir*. It came at a crucial point in his life, as he remarked in a letter written to a London correspondent in 1815: 'When I was done with my Apprenticeship, I felt just as one may suppose a Bird wou'd feel, upon escaping from its cage, the long restraints of School & business, sat heavy on my mind and made me pant for liberty and when I felt in Possession of *Her* I became like a wild thing, without either fear or foresight.'

Despite the help of various Newcastle friends, and the prospect of unlimited work, Bewick's subsequent stay in London lasted no more than nine months. His deep dislike of the city and its ways, so feelingly described in the *Memoir*, is echoed in one of the earliest of his letters to survive. It was written to his godmother's daughter, Mrs Elizabeth Hymers, before the end of 1776: '. . . I must first begin by telling you that I like it (or like to live in it) very badly – . . . but least you shou'd suspect by this that I have been out of employ – (the case with so many) I can with pleasure assure you, that is not or has not been the case . . . – yet notwithstanding all this, and 'tho I might allway continue to meet with the greatest encouragement imajinable – yet wou'd I rather live in both poverty and insecurity in NCastle. The Lord Mayor show – and all the numerous shows to be seen in London may give a momentary satisfaction – cannot afford me half the pleasure – which I allways felt in my excurtions – on the many Saturday nights and Sunday mornings – thro the pleasant Woods – to Eltringham – I find that I am, and shou'd be *deprived* (was I to continue here) – deprived of all that heart felt pleasure and satisfaction which I allways found in the many calm and contemplative walks through the pleasant Woods on my way to Eltringham . . . – You perhaps (like many of its visitors) – have only viewed it on one side – I mean that side, which is cover'd with all the porrige of outside show . . . - you might see the contrast and wou'd find it impossible to overlook the many scenes of misery – villainy – unnoticed merit – poverty – with a long list of etcetera's too tedious to mention . . .' Elizabeth Hymers' reply provides an interesting light on Bewick's sober character even as a young man, for she remarked upon her want of surprise at his reaction: 'I thought London wou'd not sute your grave turn.' His fellow-apprentice David Martin likewise wrote to him at about the same time, saying that he was sorry to hear of his dislike of the cockneys: 'although I am not much surpris'd when I consider your natural love of sincerity and simple Honesty, that you despise the Luxury Pomp and splendour of the Town and the mean and despicable methods made use of by the generality of its Inhabitants to impose on the unwary Stranger . . .'

Bewick was soon back in Newcastle, and though rather reluctantly

[15]

settled into a partnership with his former master that was to last for twenty years. It was not to be an eventful life full of dramatic incident of the sort to sustain a gripping narrative in his *Memoir*. He became too busy for travel, apart from occasional walking trips and late summer holidays by the sea at Tynemouth. By the time he was thirty-three he was most happily married and settled in a small house outside the old town walls of Newcastle with a comforting view of the open countryside to the west. This is the point at which the narrative thread in his *Memoir* begins to fade and for any detail relating to his daily life the enquirer has to turn to what can be found in the surviving correspondence. But the period of the partnership with Beilby was to see the publication of the celebrated natural histories, the *General History of Quadrupeds* on which work began in 1781 (rather earlier than recorded in the *Memoir*), and the first volume of the *History of British Birds*. The *Memoir* is clear in the reasons given for the publishing of the *Quadrupeds* – they rested on a simple desire to improve on the appalling crudity of the illustrations in all but the most expensive books on natural history. To produce a thorough and newly researched scientific text was never the purpose, though later critics have sometimes come down too severely on the book for its want of this. It was avowedly a compilation, put together for the most part by Beilby, making use of such standard texts as he could secure, but with the addition of Bewick's own observations on the creatures with which he was familiar. The two authors were surprised by the book's success which put a constant spur on them to improve the text as best they could as seven editions followed during the next thirty years.

The *History of British Birds* began to take up Beilby and Bewick's attention almost immediately after the *Quadrupeds* first appeared in 1790 – urged on by a message of encouragement from Sir Joseph Banks. Originally it was intended to produce a general work that included foreign as well as British birds. Much of Bewick's time at Wycliffe in the museum of Marmaduke Tunstall – so delightfully described in the *Memoir* and several of his letters – was eventually to be wasted, for when the scope of the original plan was clearly seen to be beyond his capacity, the many drawings he made of foreign species had to be discarded. The first volume dealing with the land birds eventually appeared in 1797, just at the end of the partnership, to be followed by a second volume on the water birds in 1804, and with this Bewick took on the complete responsibility for the text.

The *Birds* established Bewick's reputation for all time, for it inspired his finest work, not only in the principal figures, but also in the decorative

[16]

tail-pieces that enlivened every spare space in the book. Of these tail-pieces Bewick wrote an interesting note in his introduction to the last edition he saw published, in 1826: 'When I first undertook my labours in Natural History, my strongest motive was to lead the minds of youth to the study of that delightful pursuit . . . My writings were intended chiefly for youth; and the more readily to allure their pliable, though discursive, attention to the Great Truths of Creation, I illustrated them by figures delineated with all the fidelity and animation I was able to impart to mere woodcuts without colour; and as instruction is of little avail without constant cheerfulness and occasional amusement, I interspersed the more serious studies with *Tale*-pieces of gaiety and humour; yet even in these seldom without an endeavour to illustrate some truth, or point some moral . . .'

The success of the *Birds* stimulated an even wider response than the *Quadrupeds*. Correspondence began to pour in, particularly from the increasing numbers of amateurs of the subject, and as he remarks, Bewick was nearly swamped by its volume. The scientific work of Yarrell and McGillivray was still many years off. There was still much that was inexact in the classification and description of the species, and it was problems of this kind that occupied many of Bewick's correspondents. He began to find himself running a clearing house for information when he had little enough time to run a general engraving business. The figures of the *Birds* need only the briefest comparison with the work of his contemporaries and predecessors for it to be understood how strikingly fresh Bewick's must have appeared at the time. Not only was there truth in outline and animated posture, but the portrayal of the birds' natural habitat was most tellingly realised. One of the most interesting accounts of the book's contemporary effect is found in a letter the Revd. Charles Kingsley wrote to Bewick's daughter Jane, many years later: 'When your father's book on birds first came out, my father, then a young hunting squire in the New Forest, Hampshire, saw the book in London, and bought at once the beautiful old copy which was the textbook of my boyhood. He, as sportsman and field-naturalist, loved the book, and carried it with him up and down, in days when no scientific knowledge could be got – from 1805–1820; and when he was laughed at in the New Forest for having "bought a book about dickybirds" – till his fellow Squires, borrowing the book of him – agreed it was the most clever book they had ever seen, and a revelation to them – who had these phenomena under their eyes all their lives, and never noticed them.' Bewick's achievement in his natural histories is even more remarkable when we remember the circumstances of their production – not as part of the general day's work, but in brief times at the end of a long day, often by the light of a candle.

For those interested in Bewick's part in the history of wood engraving, the *Memoir* is sadly brief in its references to the technical aspects of his work. There is little space here to elaborate on the subject sufficiently to do it justice, but it cannot pass without remark. Bewick has sometimes been wrongly described as the inventor of wood engraving, when he was in fact its restorer and improver. His significance lay in the fact that he was an artist and draughtsman of subtlety and strength, blessed with an imaginative and inventive genius. His very great technical skill, trained in all aspects of the craft of a general engraver on metals – though never dominated by it, enabled him to use the same engraving tools on the end-grain of boxwood with a mastery and freedom of expression that gave his interpretation on wood a freshness and spontaneity which any reproductive engraver found impossible to match. The fact that he worked on a small scale in no way diminishes his achievement. One of the best known references to Bewick's engraving and artistry is to be found in the painter C. R. Leslie's *Hand-book for Young Painters*: 'While speaking of the English School, I must not omit to notice a truly original genius, who, though not a painter, was an artist of the highest order in his way – Thomas Bewick, the admirable designer and engraver on wood . . . The wood-cuts that illustate his books of natural history, may be studied with advantage by the most ambitious votary of the highest classes of Art – filled as they are by the truest feeling for Nature, and though often representing the most ordinary objects, yet never, in a single instance, degenerating into common-place . . . The student of Landscape can never consult the works of Bewick without improvement.'

Nearly fifteen-hundred of Bewick's preliminary pencil studies and highly finished watercolours have survived, many of them extraordinarily fine and virtually all displaying the essence of his success as an engravér. Thirty-one have been reproduced in this book. Many show the crease marks resulting from their use in transferring the subject to the woodblock surface. He blackened the back of the paper with a soft pencil, folded the drawing over the block to secure it, and then with a fine point scribed round the basic outlines only. The silvery line thus transferred served as his guide to the freehand engraving of the wood. Bewick saw the surface as a solid black, with every cut taking out white from the black ground. Inspection of any of the engravings reproduced in this book confirms the principle. Even those lines which appear as an isolated black, have none of the laborious smoothness of the careful

[18]

reproductive engraver working on either side of a previously drawn line.

Bewick's success had a far reaching effect on book illustration throughout the greater part of the nineteenth century. A process that had been thought fit only for the meanest chap-book and broadside, was given respectability. The fact that the woodblock, unlike the copper engraving, could be printed along with the text it illustrated – although considerable technical skill was required of the printer if he was to do so well – gave an added impetus to the publishers' approval of its use.

Many apprentices were trained in the workshop and about ten of these achieved some eminence in later life, for the most part in the London trade. Some of them engraved a number of the tail-pieces in the natural histories, largely based on their master's designs, and many were engaged on work that came to the shop from printers and publishers in all quarters of the country as Bewick's reputation increased. His account of the apprentices in the *Memoir* is again tantalisingly uneven, though from the correspondence and the workshop records, more can now be discovered of the extent of their contribution.

A good deal of the *Memoir* is taken up with Bewick's views on such topics as politics, pacifism and religion, and his musings on the hereafter. Some of this has been omitted in the present edition – which is not to say that these passages are without interest, for they express the man, but they have less direct appeal for the general reader. The writing of this sort clearly reflects the manner and subject matter of his convivial gatherings with his cronies at Swarley's Club and the Blue Bell in Newcastle. In fact there is a deal of good sense to be found in his views on education – which anticipated the Education Act by fifty years – the conservation of fish, bad beer, the Enclosures, and the 'chaos of religious works' and the 'waggon loads of sermons' with which he tells us his youthful mind was confused.

When the *Memoir* was eventually published in 1862, so many years after Bewick's death, Charles Kingsley wrote to his friend Thomas Dixon of Sunderland: 'You and your friends in free kindness could not have devised a present more to my taste than Bewick's Autobiography. I have read it through, and am equally delighted and astonished at it. Brought up as I was on "Bewick's Birds" . . . I always held him to be a great genius in his own line, but I was not prepared to find him so remarkable a man in other respects – his temperance and thrift, his simple virtue, his sound and wide views on all matters political and social, astonish me as do the prophecies, if I can so call them, and none more than those on social and economic reform which has since been carried out . . .'

[19]

Bewick was a kindly and loving father, although his concern for his son's health and success in life very nearly overpowered the boy's diffident nature. Robert's skill on the Northumbrian small-pipes – that charming and delicate instrument, last of the English bagpipes, which flourishes to this day – delighted his father who curiously fails to say so in the *Memoir* when recounting with much interesting detail his own part in the preservation of its music. Bewick's distrust of many of his fellow men and his too ready bearing of a grudge and imagined slights, led him into a turmoil of time-wasting disputation and litigation. But to his closer friends he was much loved and he was ever loyal to them. One of the most agreeable contemporary accounts of him in later years was that of Dr Robert Blakey: 'I did not know Thomas Bewick until within the last ten years of his life. He was then an interesting-looking old man, of portly size, and of a good-humoured and social temperament. He frequented, on certain evenings, a sort of club-room at the Fox and Lamb at the foot of Pilgrim Street, Newcastle-upon-Tyne, and many happy and pleasant hours he spent with a few select, intelligent, and jocular friends, who congregated here, chiefly with a view to enjoy his company and conversation. He was fond of porter, and I have known him sit from seven o'clock in the evening till eleven, sipping his favourite beverage to the tune of five or six pints. It did not seem to produce any muddling or stupefying effect upon him whatever. He was always clear, collected, humorous, and pleasant . . . Bewick was not what may be called a vain man of his great fame and acquirements, for pride he had none. Still, he loved to dwell with cheerful complacency upon his own exploits, and upon subjects closely connected with them . . . He could not be considered a learned man, but he possessed a more than usual share of common sense; and this generally conducted him to safe and judicious conclusions on most subjects in which he felt any interest. He was a keen observer of the world, yet his shrewdness was entirely devoid of cunning and ill-nature.'

The most vivid record of Bewick in old age was written by Audubon, the great American naturalist and artist, who visited him in 1827 while touring Britain seeking subscriptions and engravers for his *Birds of America*. Prepared as an article in his *Ornithological Biography* of 1831, it paints a moving and delightful picture of the man:

'At length we reached the dwelling of the Engraver, and I was at once shewn his workshop. There I met the old man, who, coming towards me, welcomed me with a hearty shake of the hand, and for a moment took off a cotton night-cap, somewhat soiled by the smoke of the place. He was a tall stout man, with a large head, and with eyes placed farther

[20]

apart than those of any man that I have ever seen: a perfect old English-
man, full of life, although seventy-four years of age, active and prompt
in his labours. Presently he proposed shewing me the work he was at,
and went on with his tools. It was a small vignette, cut on a block of boxwood not more than three by two inches in surface, and represented a
dog frightened at night by what he fancied to be living objects, but which
were actually roots and branches of trees, rocks and other objects bearing
the semblance of men. This curious piece of art, like all his works, was
exquisite . . . The old gentleman and I stuck to each other, he talking of my
drawings, I of his wood cuts. Now and then he would take off his cap,
and draw up his grey worsted stockings to his nether clothes; but
whenever our conversation became animated, the replaced cap was left
sticking as if by magic to the hind part of his head, the neglected hose
resumed their downward journey, his fine eyes sparkled, and he delivered
his sentiments with a freedom and vivacity which afforded me great
pleasure . . . The tea drinking having in due time come to an end, young
Bewick, to amuse me, brought a bagpipe of a new construction, called
the Durham Pipe,* and played some simple Scotch, English and Irish
airs, all sweet and pleasing to my taste . . . The company dispersed at an
early hour, and when I parted from Bewick that night, I parted from a
friend . . . I revisited him . . . on the 16th April, and found the whole family
so kind and attentive that I felt quite at home. The good gentleman,
after breakfast, soon betook himself to his labours, and began to shew
me, as he laughingly said, how easy it was to cut wood; but I soon saw
that cutting wood in his style and manner was no joke, although to him
it seemed indeed easy. His delicate and beautiful tools were all made by
himself, and I may with truth say that his shop was the only artist's
'shop' that I ever found perfectly clean and tidy.

   '. . . My opinion of this remarkable man is, that he was purely a son of
nature, to whom alone he owed nearly all that characterized him as an
artist and a man. Warm in his affections, of deep feeling, and possessed
of a vigorous imagination, with correct and penetrating observation, he
needed little extraneous aid to make him what he became, the first engraver on wood that England has produced. Look at his tail-pieces,
Reader, and say if you ever saw so much life represented before . . . As you
turn each successive leaf, from beginning to end of his admirable books,
scenes calculated to excite your admiration everywhere present themselves. Assuredly you will agree with me in thinking that in his peculiar

* A confusion of counties: Audubon meant the Northumbrian pipes, the 'new
construction' being a reference to the key-work on the pipe chanter which at
that time had not long been introduced.

[21]

path none has equalled him. There may be men now, or some may in after years appear, whose works may in some respects rival or even excel his, but not the less must Thomas Bewick of Newcastle-on-Tyne be considered in the art of engraving on wood what Linnaeus will ever be in natural history, though not the founder, yet the enlightened improver and illustrious promoter.'

NOTE ON THE TEXT

The *Memoir* has had a chequered publishing history. It first appeared in 1862, thirty-four years after Bewick's death. In transcribing and editing the manuscript, his eldest daughter Jane smoothed out the writing and omitted a number of passages – in particular the important references to his apprentices. She also had the unwelcome assistance of her cousin Robert Ward, the book's printer, who forced a number of additional adjustments. Some of the missing sections were reinstated in Austin Dobson's edition of 1887, although the basic presentation of the text remained the same. Selwyn Image introduced the 1862 text for a third edition in 1928, and in 1961 Montague Weekley introduced a fourth edition which was abridged but which in certain parts took in the results of a fresh appraisal of the manuscript. My own edition, published by the Oxford University Press in 1975, presented for the first time the complete text as Bewick wrote it; the 1979 Oxford paperback of this edition is at present still in print.

The original manuscript, which was acquired by the British Museum in 1927, remains the basis for the present edition. But while the idiosyncrasies of Bewick's spelling have been retained, his somewhat erratic punctuation has been adjusted to ease the reading; some of the contractions and the many ampersands have been spelt out, and his liberal use of capitals has been modernised. The more obvious slips of the pen and the misspellings of certain well-known names have been corrected. Although he worked from preliminary drafts, the manuscript as Bewick left it was not ready for the printer and it retains many interpolations and alternatives of word and phrase over which the editor has to exercise his own judgement. The work was given neither title nor chapter divisions: the divisions observed here are those of the first edition. The present omission of certain sections has already been referred to in the Introduction: these can be identified as Chapters 17–19 and 25–28 in the Oxford paperback of 1979.

Because the *Memoir* provides little detail relating to Bewick's day-to-day life in his later years, the reader who wishes to pursue his interest further, will find an essential supplement in *Bewick to Dovaston, Letters 1824–28*, edited by Gordon Williams, and published by Nattali & Maurice/Bodley Head in 1968: this is at present still available. The only modern biography, *Thomas Bewick*, by Montague Weekley, was published in 1953 and is now difficult to find. My own *Thomas Bewick, an illustrated record of his life and work*, Tyne & Wear County Council

Museums, 1979, is a picture book produced to record the themes of the 150th anniversary exhibition held at the Laing Gallery, Newcastle upon Tyne in 1978: it attempts to provide as wide a display as possible of the whole gamut of the Bewick engraving shop's work on metal as well as on wood; reference to some of the other earlier literature, which is extensive, can be found in its note on further reading.

1

Tynemouth, November, 1822

MY DEAR JANE

It is in compliance with your wishes, that I have after much hesitation and delay, made up my mind to give you some account of my life, as it may at a future day amuse you and your brother and sisters in your passage through its crooked, as well as its pleasant paths; and as it may also satisfy your curiosity to know something about your pedigree, I will inform you of what I have been told respecting it, as far back as I can.

My grandfather, Thomas Bewick, farmed the lands of Painshaw field and Burches Neuk, near Bywell, and also the colliery on Mickley Bank or Mickley Common – how long since I know not, but it might probably be about the year 1700. He had the character of being one of the most intelligent, active and best farmers on Tyneside, and it was said, that by his good management and great industry, he got to be very rich; and excepting his being an expert or a great angler, I know little more about him. My grandmother's maiden name was Agnes Arthur, the daughter of a laird of that name at Kirkheaton, where my father was born in the year 1715, while his mother was there (I believe) on a visit to her friends.

My maternal grandfather, Thomas Wilson and my grandmother, whose maiden name was Hannah Thompson, lived at Ainstable in Cumberland; but whether he was curate of the parish of that place, or parish clerk I do not know. It is certain however that he was one or the other, and that he taught a school there; and from the circumstance of his teaching his sons, and some of his daughters Latin, I conclude he taught some of his scholars the same language.

When he died, his eldest son, Christopher, became possessed of his freehold property, consisting of a house etc. and a few fields adjoining it. The rest of his family were left little besides a good education, and were spread abroad in the world to do the best they could for themselves. In this state of their affairs, my mother, Jane, and her youngest sister Hannah, were taken by a distant relation, a Mrs Gregson of Appleby, and remained with her untill she could get them places to live at.

About this time the Reverend Christopher Gregson had been appointed to the curacy of Ovingham, and wanted a housekeeper, and my mother, 'tho young, was thought able to undertake that office and accordingly engaged to perform it.

[25]

Your maternal grandfather's name was Robert Elliot and your grandmother's Jane Forster. He farmed the land of Woodgate near Bill Quay, where your mother was born; he afterwards removed to a farm at Ovingham, where he died in 1777, leaving the character of a sensible honest and industrious man.

How long my mother lived in Mr Gregson's place before her marriage I know not, but from him, I afterwards learned that she was a valuable servant to him, both with respect to the management in his housekeeping concerns, and also for the occasional assistance she afforded him in hearing his pupils their Latin tasks. From this place, in the year 1752, she married my father and went to live with him at Cherry-burn House, near the small village or hamlet of Eltringham, where all their family, of which I was the eldest, were born – the family consisting of myself and brothers John and William, and my sisters Hannah, Agnes, Ann, Sarah and Jane. Sarah died at the age of 16; the rest were reared to maturity or were sent off one way or another into the world.

In August 1753 I was born and was mostly intrusted to the care of my Aunt Hannah (my mother's sister) and my grandmother Agnes Bewick, and the first thing I can remember was that the latter indulged me in every thing I had a wish for, or in other words made me a great *Pet*. I was not to be snubbed (as it was called) do what I would and in consequence of my being thus suffered to have my own way, I was often scalded and burnt, or put in danger of breaking my bones by falls from heights I had clambered up to.

The next circumstance, which I well remember, was that of my being put to Mickley school, when very young, and this was not done so much with a view to my learning, as it was to keep me out of '*harm's way*'. I was sometime at this school without making much progress in learning my letters and spelling small words. The master perhaps was instructed not to keep me very close at my book, but in process of time he began to be more and more severe upon me, and I see clearly at this day, that he frequently beat me when faultless, and also for not learning what it was not in my power to comprehend. Others suffered in the same way, for he was looked upon as a severe or cross man and did not spare his rod. His name I do not recollect but he was nicknamed *Shabby Rowns*. He was a tall thin man, and with a countenance severe and grim he walked about the school room with the taws or a switch in his hand, and he no doubt thought he was keeping the boys to their lessons; while the gabbering and noise they made was enough to stun any one, and impressed the people passing by with the idea that Bedlam was let loose.

[26]

How long he went on in this way I do not recollect, but like many others of his profession, who were at that time appointed to fulfill that most important of all offices, no pains was taken to enquire into the requisite qualifications befitting them for it – and this teacher was one of that stamp. He went on with a senseless system of severity, where ignorance

and arrogance were equally conspicuous. Conduct like this sours the minds of some boys, renders others stupid and serves to make all more or less disgusted with learning.

Upon some occasion or other, he ordered me to be flogged – and this was to be done by what was called hugging, that is by mounting me upon the back of a stout boy, who kept hold of my hands over his shoulders, while the posteriors was laid bare, and where he supposed he could do the business freely; in this instance however he was mistaken for, with a most indignant rage I sprawled, kickt and flung, and as I was told, bit the innocent boy on the neck, when he instantly roared out and flung me down, and on my being seized again by the old man, I rebelled and broke his shins with my iron hooped cloggs and ran off. By this time, the boy's mother, who was a spirited woman, and lived close by, attracted by the ferment that was raized, flew (I understood) into the school room, when a fierce scold ensued between the master and her. After this I went no more to his school, but played the truant every day, and amused myself by making dams and swimming boats in a small bourne which ran through a place then called the 'Colliers-close-Wood', 'till the evening, when I returned home with my more fortunate or more obedient school fellows. How long it was before my abscense from school was discovered I know not, but I got many severe beatings from my father and mother, in the interval between my utterly leaving the school and the old master's death. As soon as another school master (James Burn) was appointed, I was sent to him and he happened to be of a directly opposite character to the late one. With him I was quite happy, and learned as fast as any other of the boys and with as great pleasure. After the death of this much respected young man, who lived

[27]

only a very few years after his being appointed schoolmaster, my learning any more at Mickley School was at an end.

Sometime after this, my father put me to school under the care of the Reverend C. Gregson of Ovingham, and well do I remember the conversation that passed between them on the occasion. It was little to my credit, for my father begun by telling him that I was so very unguideable that he could not do it, and begged of my new master that he would undertake that task, and they both agreed that to 'spare the rod was to spoil the child' – and this system was I think too severely acted upon, sometimes upon trivial occasions, and sometimes otherwise.

After being sometime kept at reading, writing and figures, how long I know not, but I know that as soon as my question was done upon my slate, I spent as much time as I could find in filling, with my pencil, all the other spaces of it, with representation of such objects as had struck my fancy, and these were rubbed out (for fear of a beating) before my question was given in. After learning figures as far as fractions and decimals etc., I was then put to learn Latin and in this I was for sometime complimented by my master for the great progress I was making – but as I never knew for what purpose it was that I was put to learn it, and was wearied out with getting off long tasks, I rather flagged in this department of my education, and the margins of my books and every space of spare and blank paper became filled with various kinds of devices or scenes I had met with and these were often accompanied with wretched rhymes explanatory of them; but as I soon filled all the blank spaces in my books, I had recourse at all spare times to the grave stones and the floor of the church porch, with a bit of chalk to give vent to this propensity of mind of figuring whatever I had seen. At that time I had never heard of the word 'drawing' being made use of, nor did I know of any other paintings, besides the King's arms in the church, and the signs in Ovingham of the Black Bull, the White Horse, the Salmon and the Hounds and Hare. I always thought I could make a far better hunting scene than the latter; the others were bejond my hand. I remember once of my master's overlooking me while I was very busy with my chalk in the porch, and of his putting me greatly to the blush, by ridiculing and calling me a conjurer. My father also found a deal of fault for 'misspending my time in such idle pursuits', but my propensity to drawing was so routed, that nothing could deter me from persevering in it, and many of my evenings at home were spent in filling the flags of the floor and the hearth stone with my chalky designs. After I had long scorched my face in this way, a friend, in compassion, furnished me with a lot of paper upon which to execute my designs. Here I had more scope – pen and ink and the juice of the brambleberry made a *grand change*. These were succeeded by a camel hair pencil and shells of colours, and thus supplied I became completely set up. But of patterns or drawings I had none – the beasts and birds which enlivened the beautiful scenery of woods and wilds surrounding my native hamlet,

furnished me with an endless supply of subjects. I now, in the estimation of my rustic neighbours became an eminent painter, and the walls of their houses were ornamented with an abundance of my rude productions, at a very cheap rate. These chiefly consisted of particular hunting scenes, in which the portraits of the hunters, the horses and of every dog in the pack, were in their opinion, *as well as my own*, faithfully delineated. But while I was proceeding in this way, I was at the same time deeply engaged in matters nearly allied to this propensity for drawing, for I early became acquainted, not only with the history and the character of the domestic animals, but also with those which roamed at large.

The conversations of the *Nimrods* of that day, in which the instincts and peculiar properties of the various wild animals were described in such glowing terms, attracted my keenest attention and to their rude and lengthened narratives I listened with extreme delight – with me they made a winters evening fly fast away. At hollyday times and at other times, when prevented by the floods of the Tyne from getting across it to school, I was sure, with the most ardent glee, to make one of the number in the hunting parties which frequently took place at that time, whether it might be in the chase of the fox or the hare, or in tracing the foumart in the snow, or hunting the badger at midnight.

[29]

The pursuing, baiting or killing these animals, never at that time struck me as being cruel – the mind had not yet been impressed with the feelings of humanity. This however came upon me at last, and the first time I felt the change, happened by my having (in hunting) caught the hare in my arms, while surrounded by the dogs and the hunters, when the poor terrified creature screemed out so pitiously, like a child, that I would have given any thing to save its life; in this however I was prevented, for a farmer well known to me, who stood close by, pressed upon me and desired I would give her to him, and from his being better able (as I thought) to save its life, I complied with his wishes; this was no sooner done than he proposed to those about him to have a 'bit more sport with her' and this was to be done by his first breaking one of its legs, and then again setting the poor animal off, a little before the dogs. I wandered off to a little distance, oppressed by my own feelings, and could not join the crew again, but learned with pleasure that their intended victim had made its escape.

The 'musical din' of the hounds still continued to have its charms and I still continued to follow them, but from that day forward I have ever wished that this poor persecuted innocent creature might escape with its life. The worrying of foxes, the baiting of foumarts, otters and badgers etc. did not awaken in me similar feelings; for in the fierce conflicts between them and the dogs, there was something like an exchange of retaliation, and not unfrequently the agressors were beaten; and I have with pleasure seen that wonderfully courageous animal the badger (with fair play) beat all the dogs of a whole neighbourhood (one after another) completely off.

In some of the vermin hunting excursions, in the depth of winter

while the whole face of nature was bound in frost and covered with deep snow, in traversing through bogs amidst reeds and rushes I have often felt charmed with the sight of birds flushed and sometimes caught by the terrier dogs, which I had never seen or heard of before, and I am still in doubt, whether some of them have not escaped being noticed as British birds. There were the diversions of the winter months, which I enjoyed the pleasure [of] in an extreme degree amidst the storm and the tempest.

In that season, I was also sometimes better employed by my attentions being engaged in looking after a small flock of sheep on the fell, a part of which flock was my own. The extremity of the weather had taught them to seek a place of shelter and this was under a steep but low brea overhung with whins, under which in such weather I was almost sure to find them and their associates all huddled together. To this place through wreaths of snow, I early bent my way, with a bundle of hay on my back and my pockets sometimes filled with oats, which I distributed amongst them. Upon these occasions, 'tho at other times extremely wild, they were quite tame and seemed to know me.* They were of the long legged, black faced kind, which were almost the only sort at that time kept in this part of the country. The *improved breed* with their fatting qualities, were then not known. The mutton of the former eat like dark juicy venison, while that of the latter puts one in mind of blubber. At that time of life every season had its charms, and I recollect well of listing with delight from the little window at my bed head, the murmuring or the roaring of the flooded burn, which passed my father's house and sometimes roused me from my bed to see what it was like. On such occasions, sometimes I would have cut a *shive* from the *black sour rye loaf* and gone to bed again to eat it. After this, my first and common employment was to muck the byer, and when the servant girl did not

* From my sheep, thus drawing into shelter, gave rise to an opinion I formed and which has been rendered more and more feasible, from long reflection, that much may yet be done to protect the largest flocks from being overblown and lost on the bleak moors, in great snow storms. Were long avenues, made by double rows of whin hedges, planted parallel to each other at about six feet asunder, and continued in the form of two sides of a square, with the whins of each side drawn together and to grow interplatted at the tops, so as to form an arched kind of roof, the sheep would, on instinctively seeing the coming storm, immediately avail themselves of such assylums and particularly in the lambing season. In the corner of the angle of this square, the shepherd might have his hovel, thatched with heather and ling, and his beds for himself and his dogs, made of the same materials; and the whole of this *beild* rendered so snug as greatly to defy the severity of the winter's drifting blasts and wreaths of snow.

come soon enough, I frequently tried my hand at milking the cows and I was always particularly keen of being there in snow storms. When this was the case, within the byer door I snugly watched the appearance of various birds which passed the little dean below, and which the severity of the weather drove from place to place in search of shelter. With the sight of my intimate acquaintances, the robins, the wrens, blackbirds, sparrows, and a solitary crow and some others, I was not much attracted, but always felt an extreme pleasure and curiosity in seeing the more rare visitants, such as the woodcock, the snipe and other waders, with the redwings and fieldfares etc. make their appearance. The winter evenings were often spent in listning to the traditionary tales and songs, relating to men who had been eminent for their prowess and bravery in the border wars, and of others who had been esteemed for better and milder qualities, such as their having been good landlords, kind neighbours, and otherwise in every respect being bold independant and honest men. I used to be particularly struck or affected with the warlike music and the songs relative to the former description of characters, but with those regarding the latter, a different kind of feeling was drawn forth, and I was often greatly distressed and often gave vent to it in a flood of tears.

These songs and *laments* were commemorative of many worthies, but the most particular ones that I now remember were those respecting the Earl of Derwent-Water, who was beheaded in the year 1715, and who was looked upon, as having been a victim to the cruelty of the reigning family, and was a young man of a remarkably good character, and who was also venerated as a saint upon earth. It was said that the light from heaven attended his corpse to the vault in Dilston Hall, and that prosperity would shine no more upon Tyneside. Then followed the sorrowful remembrances of those who were dead and gone. To sigh over them was unavailing. They had filled the space allotted to them on this side of time and the winds have blown over their silent graves for ages past. The predictions that the mansions of those who remained would soon for want of heirs become desolate – these and such like melancholly reflections made a deep impression on my mind, and I have often since with feelings of extreme regret beheld these mansions, once the seats of hospitality, delapidated, and the families which occupied them now become extinct and forgot.

When the winter began somewhat to abate of its rigours, or in the early spring, it was a common job for me before setting off to school, to rise betimes in the morning, as indeed I was always accustomed to do, and equipt with an apron, an old dyking mitten and a sharpened broken

The Beggar and his Dog at the Rich Man's Gate

The rich man's grand gateway and his distant mansion make a bitter contrast with the situation of this starving one-legged veteran of the European Wars. In the finished engraving a fine peacock graces the rich man's wall, to add to the irony. NHSN

The Blind Man and the Boy at the River Crossing

The boy leading the blind man is unable to read, and therefore fails to heed the warning sign on the rock: 'Keep on this side'. In the finished engraving the addition of a dog (who finds the correct crossing point instinctively) gives further point to the narrative. NHSN

A Suicide and his Dog

*A scene inspired by the suicide of an officer once observed by Bewick in
Benwell Down, Newcastle.* BM

A Collier Brig beached at Bill Point on the Tyne BM

sickle, to set off among the whin bushes which were near at hand, to cut off their last year's sprouts. These were laid into a corner 'till the evening, when I stripped and fell to work to *cree* them with a wooden mall in a stone trough, untill these tops of the whins were beaten to the consistancy of soft wet grass, and with this mess I fed the horses before I went to bed, or in the morning, as occasion might require. They were shy about eating this kind of provinder at first and I was obliged to mix oats with it, but they soon became so fond of it alone, that there was no nead of any mixture. I know not whether a scarcity of fodder first gave rise to the suggestion of using this expedient, or that it was tried as an experiment, but certain it is that this kind of food agreed so well with the horses that they became soon very sleek and cast their winter coat of hair, long before other horses that were fed in the common way. Cows would not eat the whin tops thus prepared (I did not indeed persist in pressing them to do so) but in a winter of scarcity I have known all hands at work in cutting ivey from the trees and even small ash twiggs, to be given to the cattle as fodder.

2

From the little window at my bed head I noticed all the varying seasons of the year, and when the spring put in, I felt charmed with the music of birds, which strained their little throats to proclaim it. The chief business imposed upon me as a task at this season, was in my being set to work to scale the pastures and medows, that is spreading the molehills over the surface of the ground. This and gardning and such like jobs was very hungry work, and often made me think dinner time was long in coming, and when, at last, it was sent to me, be what it would I sat down on the *lown* side of a hedge and eat it with a relish that neaded no sauce.

As soon as the bushes and trees began to put forth their buds and made the face of nature look gay – this was the signal for the angler to prepare his fishing tackle, and in doing this I was not behind hand with any of them in making my own all ready. Fishing rods, set gads and night lines were all soon made fit for use, and with them late and early I had a busy time of it during the long summer months and untill the frosts of autumn, forbid me to proceed. The uneasiness which my late evening wadings by the water side gave to my father and mother I have often since reflected upon with regret – they could not go to bed with the hopes of getting to sleep, while haunted with the apprehension of my being drowned, and well do I remember to this day, my father's well known whistle which called me home – he went to a little distance from the house, where nothing obstructed the sound, and whistled so loud through his finger and thumb that in the still hours of the evening, it might be heard echoing up the vale of the Tyne to a very great distance. This whistle I learned to imitate and answered it as well as I could and then posted home.

From early in morning 'till night I was scarcely ever out of an action either good or bad, or when not kept close at school, or in doing jobs, such as those I have before described, I was almost constantly engaged in some mischievous prank or other, but with a detail of these it would be wearysome to load my narrative; they were occasioned by the overflowings of an active wild disposition. At one time, in imitation of the savages described in *Robinson Crusoe* or some other savages, I often, in a morning, set off *stark naked* across the fell, where I was joined by some associates, who in like manner run about like mad things – or like Bedlamites who had escaped. Climbing the tall trees at Eltringham for rooks' nests at the hazard of breaking our necks or our bones, was another piece of business which engaged our attention. I also was engaged in another equally dangerous, and that, was by my having formed the resolution of *curing* a vicious *runaway* horse belonging to my father which none durst mount. I however took the opportunity, when out of sight of any of the family, to do so, and with my hand entwined in his mane and bare-backed, I set him agoing and let him run over sykes and burns, up hill and down hill, untill he was quite spent; and in a short time I discovered that to make him run at all, he must be whipt to it. At other times I swam him in the river, till this and such like treatment made him look ill and quite tamed him. I have often since shuddered at the thoughts of doing these and such like desperate acts, and wonder how I escaped – but neither caution or fear had at that time taken a place in the mind; on the contrary any uncommon or frightful exploit had charms in it that I could not resist. One of these pranks however, attracted the attention of the neighbourhood, brought me into a great dilemma and occasioned me a severe beating. Having engaged my constant associate, Joseph Liddell, who was ever ready at my command to help me as soon as I communicated any design to him, on this occasion I observed two oxen in a little savanna, or little bit of grazing ground, surrounded with hazel and other bushes, near the brink of the river, – thither we went in order to enjoy so tempting a sight as to see them plunge overhead into the flood. When all was ready, we suddenly, with long branches in our hands, sprung upon them from the bushes overhanging the precipiece, the danger of which they did not see, and they were plunged with such a *delightfull dash*! overhead into the river. They however happened to be no worse for it, for they were driven down by the rapid current of the flood, and landed safely at a distance below.

This exploit happening on a Sunday forenoon was an aggrevation of the crime. After this my father mostly took me with him to church – but while there, except shouting as loud as I could, while the psalms were singing, there was little to engage my attention. I therefore employed myself in almost constantly drawing various figures upon the soft-painted book board with a pin – in doing this no one noticed me, especially as I held down my head; and having got the church service off, I repeated it the same as the congregation. This apparently regular behaviour was not, however, of long duration and was broken in upon at last. Sunday after Sunday a clownish fellow had obtruded himself into our pew. I did not think this quite right and wished to put an end to it and this happened in a very rude way in the end. A dumb man ('Dummy of Wylam') a '*constant regular*' *churchman*, had a seat in the

[35]

pew before ours – where regularly during the service he fell fast asleep. In that state, and sitting right before our obtruder, I reached to aside and gave Dummy a smart blow on the head – and instantly, as if I knew nothing of the matter, seemed quite grave and intent on looking on my prayer book, while the fellow was putting on a *broad grin*. At this *poor Dummy* was so enraged, and with a distorted countenance he kept thumping the man on the face and head, making at the same time a hideous noise, which was heightened by the fellow's shouting and calling him a fool, at the same time assuring him that it was I that gave the blow and not him. To the deaf man this was a waste of words. It nead not be added that the whole congregation was greatly disturbed, while perhaps none knew or suspected the cause except my father and my preceptor in the pulpit.

Sometimes, the lads in the same class I belonged to, when we had been *doing amiss*, were sent to cut birch rods to whip us with; at other times we were locked into the belfry, where we often amused ourselves by drawing each other up by the bell ropes to the first floor, but one of our comrades who we were drawing up, having by the rope's slipping too violently through the hands of those who held it, he was precipitated to the ground, by which fall he was a good deal hurt; after this that mode of punishing us altogether was dropt. It sometimes happened to me to be confined there alone, but having got up to the top of the steeple, and whether I had ventured a little down on the outside to look after birds' nests, I do not remember, but this was asserted by some of the women in the village, who, upon the occasion found a deal of fault with the Parson for putting me into a place where such risks were to be run. Poor man, I think he had a troublesome time of it with one or another of us, and I remember well, once in particular, of putting him into very great pain and distress of mind. After a great flood a large piece of ice about the size of the floor of a room had been left in a place called 'Ned's Hole' by the side of the river. This I got upon and persuaded several others to do the same and then set to work with a *boat stower* to push it off shore, and in this manner we got to some distance up the river, opposite to the Parsonage garden, where our master happened to be and saw us. I could see by his agitated motions and his up lifted hands, that he was put into a state much easier to be felt than described. After having been guilty of misdemenours of this kind, I did not go back to school that day, but waded or other wise crossed the river, and sat down or amused myself among the bushes on the water banks, untill the rest of the scholars left school, when I joined them and went home; but as it would not have been safe for me to go to bed (if consious [of] guilt, if otherwise

[36]

betrayed) for fear of a visit from my father there, I always took up my abode for the night in the byer loft among the hay or straw – knowing well that when his passion subsided I should escape a beating from his hands.

The first cause of my preceptor's beginning a severe system of flogging (besides the quantum of it I received for mischievous acts) was for not getting off my Latin tasks. When this was not done to his mind, he by way of punishment, gave me another still worse to do and still longer, 'till at length I gave over even attempting to get through them at all, and begun to stand a flogging without being much put about by it. I

think (at this day) my very worthy preceptor, in following this rather indiscriminate system of severe punishments, was wrong, for he very often beat his own son,* a youth of an uncommonly mild, kind and cheerfull disposition, whom I often felt more distressed at seeing punished, than I felt for myself, for I mostly considered that I richly deserved the stripes inflicted upon me, and that he did not. There was another misdemeanour (above all the rest) for which I was most severely punished, either at school or at home, than for any other fault and that was for fighting with other boys. To put a stop to this practice was at the particular request of my mother – to her it was odious in the extreme. Her reasons for it I do not forget, and she quoted scripture for what she advanced in favour of her arguments – therein we were directed 'if we were struck on one cheek to turn the other also' – (I forget the exact words) but it is a portion of scripture which I did not obey. She also maintained that the business of fighting was degrading to human nature and put a man that did so, upon a level with dogs. I am conscious that I never sought a quarrel with any one, but when insulted I found it very bad to bear and mostly in the most secret or hidden manner contrived *to fight it out*.

* Christopher Gregson Esqr of Apothecaries Hall, London – he died and was buried at Ovingham [1815].

[37]

When the floggings inflicted upon me, had in a great measure begun to lose their effect, another mode was fallen upon and that was, after the school hours were over, to keep me behind and lock me into the church, where I was kept 'till the dusk of the evening. This solitary confinement was for sometime very irksome to me, for I had not at that time got over a belief in ghosts and boggles and for the sight of which, in this place I was constantly upon the look out – oppressed with fear, I peeped here and there into every corner in dread of seeing some terrible Spirit. In time however this dread abated, and I amused myself as well as I could in surveying the surrounding objects, and having at last begun to climb up the pillars, with the help of a rope or a hankerchief, as I used to do in climbing large trees, it happened one evening, when my master as usual came to let me out, that I was sitting astride upon the capital of one of the pillars, where he could not, or did not see me, when he began to call on me and I made no answer. He then posted off to see if the door was fast and having ascertained this, he marched along the aisles in great perturbation of mind, frequently exclaiming to himself, God bless me! etc. When he was gone I slipped down and found the choir door only bolted on the inside – so I waded the river and posted home and slept in my old assylum, the hay loft. I have frequently bitterly repented of having given a man who I afterwards so very highly respected through life, so much pain and trouble.

I have noticed before, the first time I felt compassion for any thing, viz. my having caught the hare in my arms. The next occurence of this kind happened with a bird – I had no doubt knocked many down with stones before, but they had escaped being taken. This time however, the little victim dropped from the tree and I picked it up; struck with its beauty, I instantly ran into the house with it – it was alive and looked me so pitiously in the face, and as I thought (could it have spoken) it would have asked me, why I had taken away its life. I felt greatly hurt at what I had done and did not quit it all the afternoon. I turned it over and over, admiring its plumage – its feet its bill and every part of it. It was a bulfinch – I did not then know its name but was told it was a 'Little Mathew Martin'. This was the last bird I killed, but many indeed have been killed since on my account. I had before been at *man fights* – dog fights and cock fights, without feeling much compassion – indeed with the last of these exhibitions, I was much more entertained at seeing the wry faces, the contortions and agitations of the clowns who surrounded the cock pit or circle, than I was at seeing the cocks fight. It was long before I felt disgusted at seeing men fight. This however happened at last. A travelling merchant, or respectable pedlar, a slim made genteel

[38]

looking man, had perhaps forgot himself over a glass and had *also* upon that occasion not minded what company he was in; he could not however be long in such company without being insulted, but be that as it may, a fight ensued, in which the stranger had been overmatched. I saw only the concluding part, and was extremely shocked at seeing it, for the stranger was sitting propped up with his arms behind him, quite spent and speechless and looked like a corpse. After sitting a short time in this helpless state, the sturdy barbarian, his opponent, walked coolly up to him, and with a blow on the face or head, laid him flat on the ground. I thought he was killed, at which I became so frantic with rage and indignation, that I believe, at the moment, if I had had a pistol at hand I would have shot him.

In going along with my narratives I have noticed some of the first impressions I felt which produced a change and left a strong sensation in my mind; in some of these the change was quick and decisive, in others of a more tardy nature, and prejudices which were early routed were not easily removed. Among the worst was that of a belief in ghosts, boggles, apparitions etc. These wrought powerfully upon the fears of the great bulk of the people at that time, and with many, these fears are not rooted out even at this day. The stories so circumstantially told respecting these phantoms and supernatural things, I listened to with the dread they inspired and it took many an effort before they could be tapered off, and I suffered much before I could do so. And what helped me very much to conquer fears of this kind was my knowing how much my father constantly scouted and despised such idle or indeed such pernitious tales – he would not allow me to plead fear as any excuse, when he had to send me [on] any errand at night, and perhaps my being frequently exposed to being alone in the dark might have the effect of

[39]

enabling me greatly to rise superiour to this kind [of] weakness. I have often had the opportunity of knowing men, both old and young, who dared to encounter any danger, yet in this way were *affraid of their own shadows* and I remember well of trying the experiment one night, upon a servant man of my father's, who was a kind of village Caesar and fear'd not to stand the most desperate battles with others of the same cast, upon every occasion. I begun by sneering at his courage, and then bet him a penny that I durst do what he dared not. All I intended I set about doing rather deliberately, and then rose up to perform *this feat* and that was only to walk along the dark passage to the back door and to repeat something (rather ominous indeed) about '*Silkey and Hedley Kow*'. After performing my task I returned with apparent agitation and fear, and sat down in silence close beside him for sometime – and then asked him if he durst do the like. I however saw by his hesitation that the performance by him was given up, and he only remarked that 'one may soon get what they'l never cast'. At another time in fair day light, I took it into my head to make another tryal of this kind, upon my father's pitmen; for this purpose I detained our cur dog, untill I buckld him up in a pair of old sods, which quite covered him beyond both his head and tail and set him off to the pit – knowing well that he would go straight there – for he was accustomed every day to leave the pit lodge and go home, where he waited untill he saw that dinner was ready, and then his reappearance at the pit was as good as telling my father and his servants to come home. I durst not have thus amused myself if I had not known that my father was out of the way – but I set off on the inside of the hedge, keeping pace with the dog, all the way up to the pit heap, near which I stopped and peeped, to see the effect that would be produced – and this was really curious. One of the men, who first saw the odd appearance of something alive with a long body, without either legs, head, or tail, moving straight forward towards him, he knew not what to make of it, and after rubbing his eyes, he ran off to his companions –

and when they had taken a peep, they all set off together with speed, on their way home.

In a business of a similar kind, which happened not long after this, it was my lot to be the sufferer. A few companions used to come at nights to *our* house to play at cards with me, and I in return visited them for the same purpose. We were however taken to task by a religious or biggoted old woman in the neighbourhood, who called the cards the 'Devil's Books', and she told me on the same night, before my setting off on this errand, that if I looked under the table I would see the Devil, and I recollect of my having several times peeped under the table that night to see if he were there. When we were done playing, two of the gamesters, as was customary set me across part of the fell towards home – I was however much surprized at their suddenly leaving me, without saying good night, or making any reply to my shouting after them, and they were [soon] out of sight. This was at a place called the 'Sandholes' which I then left and was turning towards home when behold, to my utter amazement, I saw the Devil. It was a clear moonlight night – I could not be mistaken – his horns – his great white goggle eyes – and teeth and tail and his whole person, stood fairly before me. As I stood and gazed, I thought the hair lifted the hat on my head. He stood and I stood for sometime, and I believe if he had then come up to me I must have dropped down. Certain it is, however, that desperation succeeded fear – I moved to aside and he did the same. The first thing I bethought of, or rather in an involuntary way, was getting out my *jackleg knife* and if he had then approached or laid hold on me, he to a certainty would have got himself stabbed. I then slipped off my clogs, made a run in a bending direction, and then at full speed ran directly towards home. He pursued me nearly to the door, but I beat him in the race. I had always understood, that after any person had seen a ghost or evil spirit and as soon as he or she came into a house with a fire in it, they would faint. I feared this, but I fainted none; and when my father asked me what was the matter, I told him I had seen the Devil, when he perhaps without thinking, gave me a slap [on] the head. It was not long, however, 'till this affair transpired – for the man who personated the Devil, when he met me, had been on his way to a *Kirn Supper* and was going in what was called a *guiseing*. When my father heard the whole of this trans-action he wrought himself up into a great rage, and very shortly after meeting with the man (Tom Usher) in the street at Corbridge, who had frightened me, he instantly paid him off by giving him a sound beating. When the people, who always considered my father as a remarkably peaceable man, saw him thus engaged, they expressed their surprize, but when they heard the reasons for what he had just done, they were in their turn also exasperated at him, and I was given to understand he was obliged to leave that village.

The first time that I took any notice of any of my female school-fellows, arose from a reproof I met with, and the manner it was given, from one of them – the amiable person alluded to was Miss Betty Gregson, my preceptor's daughter and somewhere about my own age. She kept a messet dog, and the sleek fat useless animal was much disliked by me, as well as by some of the other boys; it having, as it sometimes did, made its appearance in the churchyard – we set about freight'ning it. For this purpose, some of us met it at every gate and outlet, and stopt its retreat, 'till it became quite distressed. This and such like was often sport to us. The last time that this kind of sport was practised upon her little dog, I happened to be the only actor. Having met with it at a little distance from its home, I stopped it from its entering the house and pursuing it about and about, or meeting it at the end of every avenue – 'till it was put into great *bodily fear*. This behaviour towards her little favourite was very offensive to Miss Greg-son. She could endure it no longer and called me to an account for it, and I can never forget her looks upon the occasion. She no doubt intended to scold me, but the natural sweetness of her disposition soon shewed itself in its true colours to me – and also that she did not know how to scold – for after some embarrassing attempts at it and some hesitations, she put me in mind of my being related to her, and of her uniform kindness to me, and with irresistable arguments and per-suasions made me see the impropriety of my conduct. With me this left its mark, for from that time forward I never plagued any of the girls at school, nor did any thing that might give them offence; nor was this impression ever afterwards effaced from my mind but has been there fostered through life and settled into a fixed respect and tender regard for the whole sex.

Hitherto my whole time at school and at home, might be considered as a life of warfare, and punishments of various kinds had been inflicted upon me apparently to litte effect. As a cure for my misdeeds, my worthy master, however, at length found out a better and a more effectual way – he one day invited me to dine with him and after shewing me the greatest kindness, he followed this up in a friendly, plain and open way, of remonstrating with me, on the impropriety of my long past bad conduct, and the evil tendancy of it together with the pain and trouble I had given him, urging me at the same time, in such a persuasive tone, instantly to desist from it, that I felt quite overpowered with this discourse and then fell into a flood of tears. This however did my business, for I never durst encounter another of this kind of his friendly meetings – and while I remained at his school, he never more had occasion to find fault with me.

After this time, many of the transactions in which I became engaged, afforded me more pleasurable recollections than those I have before described, and as silent time stole away in the varied seasons of the long-measured years, changes gradually took place in many of the erroneous notions I had formed of things; and as the mind became more expanded, curiosity led me to enquire into the nature of the objects which attracted my attentions. Among the first was that of the birds, their nests, their eggs and their young and these to me were long a source of great delight – and many a spring morning I watched and looked after them; and many a summer's evening, on my way home from school, I spent lost in wonder, in examining the works going forward among a nation of

pismires (ants). The place they occupied, was on the top of the 'Boat Hill' near Eltringham, and it was the largest I ever saw. From it their narrow roads through the grass, radiated in various directions to a great distance – these were like as many turnpike roads, and as busily crouded as any among men leading from or to a great faire. As an experiment to see what effect might be produced, I sometimes with a stick over-turned the accumulated gatherings of the stores of the whole nation, on which ensued to them the greatest bustle and confusion, and next morning I beheld with surprize every thing apparently restored to the same order, as before I disturbed them.* I observed they had other enemies that

* Ants. The history and œconomy of these very curious insects are (I think) not well known – they appear to manage all their affairs, with as much forethought and greater industry than mankind; but, to what degree their reasoning and instructive powers extend is yet a mistery. After they have spent a certain time toiling on earth, they then change this abode, get wings, and soar aloft into the atmosphere. It is not well known what state they undergo, before they assume this new character, nor what becomes of them after.

broke in upon them and which perhaps injured them more than I had done – and these were the turkeys from the village, where great numbers were bred every year. As soon as the young brood were able to walk abroad, the mother led them every day to this great ant hill, where they no doubt made terrible havoc in destroying both their works and the inhabitants.

Bees also attracted much of my attention; I could not see into the interior of their works, but made every enquiry of those who had long kept them, and gathered, in this way, as good a knowledge of their history and economy as I at that time could; and one of my morning jobs was to sit before the hives with a stick like a spatula, to kill the wasps as they alighted to enter and rob them. I could see the bees enter, loaded with what they had culled from every flower but never could see them attack or repel their enemies.

I also long amused myself in observing the constant *murders* of a large spider, in his web, placed in a corner of the little window at my bed head. This I prevented the servant girl from brushing away, being wishfull to see how he managed his affairs, and these did not excite in me any favourable opinion of the successfull murderer – having long seen him seize every innocent fly that set foot on his snares, I had a mind to try how he would conduct himself towards a more powerfull opponent. For this purpose, I caught a wasp, which I held by its wings upon the web, untill its feet got entangled, when out came the hitherto unthwarted tyrant, and after some apparent hesitation, he at length was tempted to pounce upon the obtruder – the struggle was however very short, for I soon saw the wasp double itself up and dart its sting into the body of its enemy – who instantly retired – and I never afterwards saw the spider make his appearance again. This is only one experiment, and further trials of this kind might be made to come at truth.

3

Cherry-bourne House, the place of my nativity, and which for many years my eyes beheld with cherished delight – is situated on the south bank of the Tyne, in the County of Northumberland, and about a quarter of a mile from the river. The house, stables etc are situated on the west side of the little dean and burn* whose bank was embellished with a number of plumb trees and terminated with the garden on the north of them. Near the house were two large ash trees, from one root but the top of one of them was blown away in a high wind, and another one, of the same kind, at a little distance from them. At the south end of the premises, was the spring well, overhung by a large hawthorn bush, behind which was a holly hedge, and bejond this again was a little boggy dean with underwood and trees of different kinds. Near the termination of this dean, towards the river, was a good many remarkably tall small ash trees and one of oak, supposed to be one of the tallest and straightest in the kingdom. On the tops of these was a rookery, the sable inhabitants of which, by their consultations and cawings and the bustle they made when building their nests were among the first of the feathered race to proclaim the approaching spring. To the eastward were cornfields and pastures, mostly surrounded with very large oaks and some ash trees – indeed at that time the country between Wylam and Bywell was beautified with a great deal of wood, which presented the appearance of a continued forest, but these are long since stubbed up – needy gentry care little about the beauty of country and part of it now is comparatively as bare as a mole hill.

To the westward, adjoining the house, lay the common or fell, which extended some few miles in length and of various breadths. It was mostly fine greensward or pastureage, broken or divided indeed, with clumps of *blossomed* whins, fox-glove, fern and some junipers, and to the westward with hether in profusion sufficient to scent the whole air. By the sides of the burns, which *guttered* its sides or scouped out hollow *gills* were seen the remains of old oaks, hollowed out by time – with alders willows and birch which were often to be met with in the same state, and these seemed to me to point out the length of time that these domains had belonged to no one. On this common, the poor man's

* This bourne formerly was supplied by a copious spring of fine water but it found its way into some pit workings and disappeared and is now only fed by day water from the fields.

[45]

heritage for ages past, where he kept a few sheep or a Kylo cow and perhaps a flock of geese and mostly a stock of bee hives – it was with infinite pleasure that I long beheld the beautifull wild scenery which these exhibited, and it is with the opposite feelings of regret that I now find all these are swept away.* Here and there on this common were to be seen the cottage, or rather, hovel, of some labouring man, built mostly at his own expense with his own hands, and to this he always added a garth and a garden upon which great pains and labour were bestowed to make both productive, and for this purpose not a bit of manure was suffered to be wasted away on the *lonnings* or publick roads. These various concerns excited the attention and the industry [of] these hardy occupants, which enabled them to prosper, and made them despise being ever numbered among the parish poor. These men and their offspring might truely be called 'a bold pesantry, their country's pride' – their children were neither pampered nor spoiled, and to this day (when grown up to manhood) I think I see their broad shoulders and their hardy sun burnt looks, which altogether bespoke the vigour of their constitutions. These cottagers (at least those of them I knew) were of an honest and independant character while, at the same time, they held the neighbouring gentry in the greatest estimation and respect, and these again in return did not overlook them but were interested in knowing that they were happy and well. Most of these poor men, from their having little intercourse with the world, were in all their actions and behaviour truly original. Except reading the Bible, local histories and old ballads, their knowledge was generally limited – and yet one of these, 'Will Bewick', from being much struck with my performances which he called pictures, became exceedingly kind to me, and was the first person from whom I gathered a kind of general knowledge of astronomy and of the magnitude of the universe. He had, the year through, noticed the appearances of the stars and the planets, and would discourse *largely* on the subject.

I think I see him yet, sitting on a mound or seat, by the hedge of his garden, regardless of the cold, and intent upon viewing the heavenly bodies, pointing to them with his large hands and eagerly imparting his knowledge to me, with a strong voice, such a one as one now seldom

* This Fell or common containing 1852 A[cres]–2 R[ods]–9 P[erches] was divided in 1812. By this division, the poor man was rooted out and the various mechanics of the villages, deprived of all benefit from it. The neighbouring farmers who reared their young cattle and kept as many sheep upon it as they pleased – must now pay rent for the allotments laid to their farms. The wisdom which dictated this change is questionable, but the selfish greediness of it quite apparent.

[46]

hears. I remember well with being much struck with his appearance –
his stern-looking brows – high cheek bones – quick eye and longish
visage, and at his resolution (upon another occasion) when he determined upon risking his own life to save that of another man. This man,
in the employ of my father, while at work as a pitman, had lost his way
in the coal workings and was a wanting, for perhaps a day or two (my
father being from home) when our old neighbour, just described, who
was also a pitman and knew the workings, equipt himself with every
thing he thought necessary for so hazardous an undertaking, and when

he was about to go down the pit shaft, I felt much distressed at seeing
my mother trembling in great agitation of mind, for the safety of both
him and his lost associate. After travelling and traversing through the
old workings of the colliery, for a long time – so long that it was feared
he had also lost himself – he however found the man alive at last, when
with his well known thundering voice, from the bottom of the shaft, he
called 'All's Well' – to the inexpressible joy of all who now crouded the
pit *heap* or surrounded its mouth.

Another of our fell-side neighbours, Anthony Liddell, was a man of
a very singular character – he might truely be said to be like no one
besides himself, and was noticed as such by the whole neighbourhood;
but a full account of him would far exceed the bounds I wish to set to
my narratives. He might indeed be called 'the village Hampden'. The
whole cast of his character was formed by the Bible, which he had read
with attention thro' and through. Acts of Parliament which appeared to
him to clash with the laws laid down in it, as the word of God, he treated

[47]

with contempt. He maintained that the fowls of the air, and the fish of the sea were free for all men; consequently game laws, or laws to protect the fisheries, had no weight with him. He would not, indeed, take a salmon out of the locks on any account, but whatever he could catch with his click-hook in the river, he deemed his own. As to what he could do in shooting game, he was so inexpert that he afforded to sportsmen many a hearty laugh at his aukwardness, for he could shoot none 'till he fixed a hay fork in the ground to rest his piece upon – in that way the very birds themselves might, by a stretch of imagination, be supposed also to laugh at him – but his deficiencies did not deter him from traversing over the countryside, as eagerly as other sportsmen, notwithstanding his want of success. Whatever he did in this way, was always done in open day, for as he feared no man, he scorned to sculk or to do any thing by stealth. The gaol had no terrors for him, for he lived better there than he did at home, and on one occasion of his being confined, when he returned home, he expressed his surprize to his neighbours, that all the time he was there '*he had not a single hand's turn to do*' and exulted not a little that the opportunity was thus given him of again reading the Bible through and through. He was a great reader of histories, especially those parts where wars and battles were described, and in any meetings with his neighbours he took the lead in discourses founded on his knowledge of this kind. Besides the Bible, Josephus was his next favourite author; next *The Holy Wars,* and these and Bishop Taylor's sermons composed his whole library, and his memory enabled him nearly to repeat whatever he had read. His deportment and behaviour were generally the reverse of any thing like sauciness, but except in ability and acquirements which indeed commanded his respect, he treated all men as his equals. When dressed, he always wore a second hand black coat; in other respects he was like no other person – in what King's reign his hat had been made was only to be guessed at, but the flipes of it were very large, and his wig was of the large curled kind, such as were worn about the time of the revolution, with a waistcoat or doublet made of the skin of some animal, and buckskin breeches turned black and glossy with long wear and of the same antiquated fashion as the rest of his apparel. Thus equipt, and with his fierce look, he made a curious figure before the Justices of the Peace and these together with his always (when summonzed before them) of undauntingly pleading his own causes, often afforded many of them so much amusement, that it was difficult for them to keep their gravity; others of them of a more grave deportment made use of threats to make him behave more respectfully – these he never failed to shew that he

[48]

The Cuckoo N H S N

The Bullfinch B M

The Wren NHSN

The Greenfinch BM

despised, and on one occasion of this kind, he told the Justice that 'he was not a bit *flaid* of him' – that there was '*nobbit yen* place that he was *flaid* of and that was Hell, and he could not send him there'. After this quarrell he was ordered out of court. He waited below in expectation of the Justice's following him to have the matter settled by a fight, and desired a gentleman to tell the Justice that he waited for him for that purpose; when he was told he had behaved insolently to him – 'oh Sir' said he (spitting into his hands), 'tell him to come here – he does not know what a fellow (aw is) I am'.

Another of our neighbours, Tom Forster, was of a different character from the last, but singular enough in his way. He was distinguished for his frugality and industry, and always shewed a wish to be looked upon in a respectfull light. He used to call at our house on a Sunday afternoon, for the purpose of having a bit of chat or conversation, with my father and mother. He took a liking to me and would observe that 'tho I was mischivous enough, yet he never heard, nor could see that I was '*parrentory*', that is, impudent or saucy, with any one. Besides this part of the good opinion he had formed, he must have had a confidence as to my keeping his secrets which he imparted to me. He kept a few sheep, on the fell and in pretence of looking after these, his secret and main business was looking after his bees; of these he had a great number of hives, all placed in very hidden and very curious situations. The narrow entrances to all of these were at some distance from the hives. Some of these apiaries were placed under the bounder hedge of the common, surrounded and hidden from sight by a great extent of old whin bushes, and besides, the hives were sheltered under the branches of the old thorns and almost quite covered or over hung by brambles, woodbine and hip bryars, which, when in blossom, looked beautifully picturesque, while at the same time they served to keep the eye from viewing the treasures thus concealed beneath.

Others of his hives were placed in the midst of a 'whin rush', that is, a great extent of old whins, the stems of which were about the thickness of a man's arm. His entrance to these was always by a *smout hole* or small opening, through which we crept on hands and knees to the hives, and which on our leaving them, the entrance was always stopped up by a bushy topped whin. He also, by way of taking off the attention of the *over-inquisitive* as to his stock of honey, kept hives in his garden at home and sold the produce of them to his neighbours, while the greater quantity was all sold at distant parts of the country. In this way and by his industry and good management in other ways, he got to be, what was accounted very rich, and as prosperity excites envy, people of that

disposition, in a kind of derision (his mother being a midwife) always called him 'Tom Howdey'.

I might swell the list of such like characters among the unoticed poor, as those I have described, but I think it would perhaps be tedious, allthough I think it a pity that such were not better known to some of the unthinking *Great*, as it might take off some of that *hauteur* which is too often shewn towards them.

Another of these uncultivated singular characters, while it exhibits human nature left to the guidance of its uncontrolled will, may be found sometimes, from the force of innate natural pride, to soar above every meanness. This man, 'tho clothed in rags, was noticed for his honour and integrity, and whose word was considered to be as good as a £1000 bond. He was one of my father's workmen, either as a pitman, a labourer or a sinker, and was of so hardy a constitution, that he thought it no hardship in a cold frosty morning, to be let down to the bottom of a sinking pit, where he was to be up to the middle or perhaps to his breast, in water, which he was to lave all away into buckets, to be drawn up to the top; but in every job he undertook, he endured its hardships without ever grumbling or thinking it so. His living was of the poorest kind, bread, potatoes and oatmeal was the only provender he kept by him; with these and milk and water he finished his meals. When, by this mode of living, he had saved the overplus money of his wages, for a month or 6 weeks, he then posted off to Newcastle to spend it in beer, and this he called '*lowsening his skin*'. When this was done, he commonly borrowed two shillings of me, to set him home again, and in this irrational way of life he continued for many years. On one occasion, when changing his beer house, and taking up his quarters in another, he had made no stipulations with his new landlord, as to the place where he was to sleep at night, and judging of him by his ragged appearance, he was thought not fit to be trusted as an inmate, without enquiring into his character, and for this purpose I was applied to by the landlord, whom I satisfied by assuring him, that notwithstanding the outward appearance of his singular looking guest, he might be trusted safely with any thing, even with untold gold, and further, that the man who could sleep upon the fallen leaves in a wood, wanted no bed in his house better than the wooden seats in his boxes, and that these would be as comfortable a bed for him as he wished for. Matters being now perfectly understood and settled, he was permitted on this, and on all future occasions during his rambles, to make this house his home. He had been but a short time in this happy assylum, untill he got a pretty numerous acquaintance, but particularly with the tradesmen who frequented the house, to whom his singularity, his droll and witty stories, and his songs, often afforded most of them great entertainment. Old age however, overtook him at last, and he was then obliged to seek parish or township relief. On this occasion a neighbouring laird persuaded him that his settlement was upon Eltringham, and got him to swear to it. When he called upon the farmers there for his pittance, they convinced him that he had sworn to what was false. He was much shocked at what he had done, and never having called upon them for his pay, they asked him why he had not done so. 'No,' said he, 'I would sooner have this hand cut off, or be found dead on the highway through want, than claim, or receive from any one, money to which I was not justly entitled.' After this he wandered away from Eltringham and took up his abode in the glasshouse at Bill Quay, where he did any little jobs in his power, and at the same time made himself very agreeable and often very entertaining to the workmen, who long remembered Johnny Chapman. From this place he set off on a visit to a friend at some distance, when he was rather unwell and not very able to undertake such a journey – and was found dead on the road between Morpeth and Newcastle.

(*Thus far was written at Tynemouth 10 December 1822*)

[51]

Before taking leave of these hardy inhabitants of the fells and wastes, whose hovels were surrounded with whins and heather, I must observe that they always appeared to me, notwithstanding their apparent poverty, to enjoy health and happiness in a degree surpassing that of most other men. Their dayly fare was commonly coarse bread, potatoes, oatmeal porridge and milk, and was only varied by their boiling the pot with animal food cabbage or other succulent vegetables and broth, on the Sundays. When tired at night with labour, having few cares to perplex them, they lay down and slept soundly, and arose refreshed from their hard beds with vigour, early in the morning.

After I left the country, I always felt much pleasure in revisiting them, and over a tankard of ale to listen to their discourse. It was chiefly upon local biography, in which they sometimes traced the pedigree of their neighbours, a long way back; and when good eating became the subject of their discourse and in telling what they liked best, one man would declare, that *ower all fruit that grew he liked potatoes and cabbage the best*, while another would press upon the audience, the deliciousness of potatoes and onion sauce, and in the warmth of his loyalty, wished that the King did but know how good a dish this was, he believed he would never want it for his supper.

With the aged men in the neighbourhood, I felt very much amused at the avidity with which they gathered news – *they seemed to live upon it*. Several of them met every day in the *Ludge* (or earth built hovel)* close by my father's pit, for the purpose of being gratified in this way. The carts and wains came in all directions, and many of them from a great distance, for coals, the drivers of which imparted to them all they knew of what was going on in their several neighbourhoods. In this kind of treat I often partook with them, when I was gin driver, by slipping in among them, between the drawing up of each cart of coals to the *bank*. The information thus obtained by our neighbours, was then speedily given in detail at the smith's shop at Mickley, whence it was spread over the neighbouring country. One of these, a very old man, John Newton (the laird of the Neuk) almost every morning, while I was very young, met me and the rest of the scholars, going to Mickley school, at or near the *Hally Well* (holy well) and he seldom passed me without clapping my head, accompanied with some good wishes. Many years after this, while I lived at the Forth, in Newcastle, I met a little boy, one morning

* This Lodge having always a good fire kept on in it, with two beds of straw, on each side bounded by two old trees to answer the double purpose of bed stocks and seats – often proved a comfortable assylum to the benighted, weary, shivering traveller, wandering on the road.

[52]

coming to school there, when I clapped his head, and hoped he was a good boy. I had not long passed from him 'till I was rather struck with the coincident recollection of his grandfather's grandfather (above named) so long before having passed me in the same way.

To these I must add another description of men, scattered about the neighbourhood, with whose history and narratives, I at that time felt greatly interested – their minute account of the battles they had been engaged in, with the hardships they endured and their hair breadth escapes, told with so much enthusiasm and exultation, emparted the same kind of feelings to me. This was long before I had reasoned myself into a detestation of war – its cruelty, its horrors and the superlative wickedness of the authors of it. I had not pictured to my mind the thousands and tens of thousands of men in their prime, being pitched against a like number of other young men, to whom they could have no enmity – to murder each other!! For what? It is foreign to my purpose to enlarge upon this subject – I must leave that for others, of my mind, to do – and there is an abundant scope to dilate upon and to depicture its

horrors in their true colours. The old soldiers, above alluded to, were mostly the descendants of the borderers, whose propensity for war might perhaps be innate. I think, however, that the breed is thinned, from the numbers that have been killed off in our Wars. One of these (a near relative) would describe his having had his knapsack shot through and through, as well as his coat laps and the cocks of his hat, and yet escape unhurt; and others of them would give a similar descriptive account, and when a party of them met over their ale, it is not easy to depicture the warmth with which they greeted each other and prided themselves on the battles they had won. One of these, during a walk, in which I fell in with him, from Newcastle to Ovingham, described the minute particulars of the battle of Minden and how, in the abscence of Lord Sackville, they shook hands, the whole length of the line, vowing to stand by each other without flinching. This tall stout man, John

[53]

Cowie, 'tho old, appeared in all the vigour of youth – he lived at Ovington; but his associate Ben Garlick, of Prudhoe, appeared as if his constitution had been broken down. They had served in a corps called Napier's Granadiers. Cowie appeared occasionally in his old military coat etc as long as he lived, and after he died this coat, which had been shot at, both at Minden and else where, was, at last hung up, on a stake on the corn rigs as a scare crow. This ferocious people formerly bore nearly the same names, on both sides of the Borders and their character seemed like a distinct people from both their English and Scottish neighbours, and war and rapine had long been their almost constant employment. Many of these, the retainers of the chieftains of old, whose iron hands were grasped, and whose feet were swift to shed blood, were called by names, descriptive of their characters and persons – which nicknames were mostly continued by their offspring, and these consisted of a great variety, both of cunning and ferocious birds and beasts, as well as some names, the meaning of which is now unknown. There were among them the hawk, glead, falcon, fox, wolf, bloodhound, greyhound, raven, crow, gorfoot, crowfoot etc.

The farmers in the neighbourhood, at the early period which I have been describing, always appeared to me, to be not of so intelligent a cast as the poor labouring man – their minds being more exclusively occupied with the management of their farms and they read but little. They were mostly of a kind and hospitable disposition, and well intentioned plain plodding men, who went jogging on, in their several occupations, as their fathers had done before them.

The next advance in society bejond these were the country lairds, who lived upon their own lands. I have always through life, been of opinion, that there was no business of any kind, nor any employment whatever, that could be compared with that of a man's farming his own land. It appeared to me that every earthly pleasure, with health and happiness, was more within his reach, than fell to the lot, of other men – but in these my notions of their happiness, I have very often seen and felt that I was grievously mistaken, for numbers of these men were grosly ignorant, and in exact proportion to that ignorance, they were sure to be offensively proud. This led them to attempt appearing above their station, which hastned them on to their ruin; but indeed, this disposition and this kind of conduct, leads to the same results with all men of this stamp. There were many of these lairds on Tyneside, as well as many who held their lands on the tenure of 'suit and service' and were nearly on the same level as the lairds. Some of the latter, lost their lands (not fairly I think) in a way they could not help, while the former by their

[54]

misdirected pride and folly, were driven into towns to slide away into nothingness and to sink into oblivion, while their old *Haa Houses* (Halls) that ought to have remained in their families from generation to generation for ever; but these, with their forgotten ancient owners, have also mouldered away. I have always felt extremely grieved to see the ancient mansions of too many of the gentlemen of the country, from somewhat similar causes meet with a similar fate.

The gentry of the country ought in an especial manner, to shew by their conduct that they are guarded against shewing any symptoms of foolish pride, and at the same time that they soared above every meanness and that their conduct was guided by truth integrity and patriotism. If they wish the people to partake with them in these good qualities they must set them the example without which, no real respect can ever be paid to them by people in the lower stations of life. Gentlemen ought never to forget the respectable station they hold in society, and that they are the natural guardians of public morals and may with propriety be considered as the head and the heart of the country, while a bold peasantry, are in truth the arms, the sinews and the strength of the same, but when these are degraded they soon become dispirited and mean and often dishonest and useless.

I think the late Duke of Northumberland, must have had an eye to raising the character of the peasantry, when he granted them small portions of land, at a reasonable rate. If so, in my way of judging, he was an honour to the pearage, and set an example worthy of himself, and worthy of imitation. By going a step further and planting healthy strong men and women on these spots, his patriotism would have been *crowned with immortality* – for I cannot help thinking, that if the same pains were taken in breeding mankind, that gentlemen have bestowed upon the breeding of their dogs, horses and game cocks, that human nature might, as it were, be new modelled, hereditary diseases banished, and such a race of mankind might people the country as we can form no true conception of; and instead of a nation of mongrels, there would, in time, appear a nation of *'Admirable Crichtons'*. If the lands commonly attached to townships, had been continued as such, or let in small portions, to mechanics and labourers, (as the late Duke had done) instead of dividing them by *Act of Parliament* among those who had already too much, the good effects to the community at large would have soon been felt; and in addition to this, if saving banks and benefit societies were encouraged by every possible means, there would be little occasion for poor laws, except as a provision, for helpless children and the lame and the blind. By such means as these, perhaps this national

[55]

evil might be done away. All men ought to provide for the necessities of old age, and be made sensible of the manly pleasure of being independant. It is degrading and in most cases disgraceful to those who look to parish assistance after a life spent in laziness and mismanagement.

I must not omit noticing a circumstance that happened to Eltringham while I was a boy. It was to have been called 'little Birmingham' but this was not accomplished. In 17–– a person of the name of Laidler, who was said to have amassed a large fortune in London, came to the north and established the iron works at 'Busy Cottage' near Newcastle, and, on his taking a view of Tyne side, he fixed upon Eltringham as a place at which he could carry on works to a much greater extent. This work he set about in great haste – all kinds of workmen were gathered together for the purpose of speedily accomplishing what he had in view, and while some of them were busy in making the mills and machinery, others were digging a mill race of about a quarter of a mile in length. But lo! when this was done, it was found (not being permitted to encroach upon the bed of the river) they had not, it was said, much more than about a foot of waterfall, and as the sides of the mill race was cut perpendicularly about two yards deep through the dark fine soil – the first great flood of the Tyne, by the sides falling in, nearly levelled and filled it up. The houses in and about the place, that had got licences to sell ale etc, were obliged to shut them up and decline – and among the rest, my father's house; and its sign of the Seven Starrs, hung up between the two ash trees, was taken down. The projector made our house his home while the works were going on and the men were paid their wages there. All was as suddenly sold off, as it was begun, and my father came to some loss, after all the turmoil and trouble he had been put to.

4

Being now nearly fourteen years of age and a stout boy, it was thought time to set me off, and my father and mother had long been planning and consulting what business it would be best to put me to, in which they were greatly at a loss what to fix upon. Any place where I could see pictures, or where I thought I could have an opportunity of drawing them, was such only as I could think of. A Newcastle bookseller whose windows were filled with prints, had applied to Mr Gregson for a boy and when I was asked if I would like to go there, I readily expressed my hearty consent, but upon my father's making every enquirey respecting this man, he was given to understand that he bore a very bad character – so that business was soon at an end.

The same year 1767, during the summer, William Beilby and his brother Ralph, took a ride to see their intimate acquaintance, Mrs Simons at Bywell, who was my godmother and the widow of the late vicar there. She gave them a most flattering account of me, so much so that they, along with her and her daughter (afterwards Mrs Hymers) all set off that afternoon to Cherry-burn to visit us and to drink tea. When the Newcastle visitors had given an account of their paintings, enamellings, drawings and engravings etc, with which account I felt much pleased, I was asked which of them I would like to be bound to, and liking the look and deportment of Ralph the best, I gave the preference to him. Matters bearing upon this business being slightly talked over, and my grandmother's having left me £20 for an apprentice fee, it was not long before something of a good understanding between parties took place, and I soon afterwards went to R. Beilby upon trial. The first of October was the day fixed uppon, for the binding. The eventfull day arrived at last, and a most grievous day it was to me – I liked my master, I liked the business, but to part from the country and to leave all its beauties behind me, with which I had all my life been charmed in an extreme degree, and in a way I cannot describe – I can only say my heart was like to break, and as we passed away, I inwardly bid farewell, to the whinney wilds – to Mickley Bank, the Stob Cross hill, to the water banks, the woods, and to particular trees, and even to the large hollow old elm which had lain (perhaps) for centuries past, on the haugh near the ford we were about to pass and had sheltered the salmon-fishers while at work there, from many a bitter blast. This old tree was swept away by the great flood of the 17 November 1771.

[57]

We called upon my much esteemed schoolfellow 'Kit Gregson' at Ovingham, where he and his father were waiting to accompany us to Newcastle, all on the same errand. We were both bound that day. While we were condoling – comforting each other – I know not what to call it, at the Parsonage gates, many of the old neighbours were assembled at the churchyard wall, to see us set off and to express their good wishes; and among the rest, to watch our departure, was a good sensible old woman of the village, named Betty Kell, for the purpose of giving both of us her blessing, and each a penny for good luck. This being done, our

horses were mounted and we commenced our journey. The parties kept at a little distance from each other. I suppose our late preceptor was lecturing his son and my father was equally busied in the same way with me. He had always set me the example and taken every opportunity of shewing how much he detested meanness, and of drawing forth every particle of pride within me, for the purpose of directing it in this way. He began and continued a long while on subjects of this kind, and on the importance and the inestimable value of honour and honesty, and urgently pressed upon me to do my duty to my master, in faithfully and obediently fulfilling all his commands – to be before-hand in meeting his wishes – and in particular to be always upon my guard in listening to the insinuations and the wicked advice of worthless persons, who I would find ever ready to poison my ear against him. He next turned his discourse on another topic, new to me from him, of great importance – Religion – and pressed this also upon me in a way I did not forget. He begged I would never omit, morning and evening addressing myself to

[58]

my maker and that, if I ceased to do so, then he believed and feared, every evil would follow it. I was greatly surprized to hear him dwell on this subject, for I think it was the first time. He used indeed to go to church, but I do not recollect his ever commenting upon the sermons he heard there, further than that the good man's discourse from the pulpit seemed to him to be wasted upon the great majority of his audience, and of his calling some of them 'holy professors'. My mother, who was of a religious turn, had indeed all her life endeavoured to make me so too, but as I did not clearly understand her well intended lectures, they made little impression. My father's pithy illustrations, as before hinted at, were much more forcably and clearly made out. I understood them well and their effect operated powerfully upon me.* I have often reflected since upon the very high importance and of the necessity of instilling this species of education into the minds of youth, for were pains taken to draw forth the pride, naturally implanted in their minds, for the wisest and best purposes, if properly directed, it would exalt human nature, and be of the utmost importance to individuals and to society. It is the want of this and the want of industry that occasions and spreads misery over the land; and how can I doubt it, if my father had been a thief, that I would not have been one also; and if a highwayman and robber, that I might not have been as expert a one as himself.

In my opinion there are two descriptions of person, who ought to forbear, or to be prevented from marrying – viz those of a base, wicked and dishonest character, and those who have broken down their constitutions by diseases, and debased both mind and body by their illicit and impure connections and dissipated lives. The latter entails misery upon their innocent tainted ofspring; and the former by the bad examples they shew to their children which grows upon them with their growth, 'till they are perfected in their wickedness and they become a curse to the community in which they live.

When we arrived at the Cock Inn, Newcastle, the documents were soon made ready to bind my companion and myself. He was bound to Messrs Doughty and Wiggins, Chemists and Druggists; but Mr Beilby

* I recollect one instance where I felt the force of this species of education. I might enumerate some others, but this left its *mark upon me*. Having fallen in with and joined two untutored lads, in Prudhoe lonning, they jumped over the hedge and filled their pockets with potatoes. The farmer was watching, but they escaped. Not having followed their example, I did not offer to fly, but he seized me and threatened what he would do; at this I was extremely distressed and had it not been that I consoled myself with the certainty that my father and mother would believe me on my asserting that I had not stolen any of his potatoes, I believe I would have drowned myself.

(perhaps from his having heard of some unfavourable account of me) and my father not readily agreeing upon the exact terms of my servitude, some fears were entertained that the business between us might be broken off. On this occasion my preceptor interfered very ardently – spoke warmly in my praise, and dwelt forcibly in particular, (notwithstanding my boyish wild behaviour at school) upon my never being saucy or sulky, nor in the least indulging in any thing like revenge. In this business Mr Gregson was ably seconded by his relation and my kind friend Joseph Langstaffe of Newcastle, who was also accuainted with my new master, and so the business of binding was settled at last.

My new master, who I believe had laid down plans for the regulation of his own conduct through life, begun with me upon a system of riged discipline, from which he never varied nor relaxed, and it was not long before I gave occasion to his putting it in force. Having walked out on a Sunday afternoon, to see the environs of the town, the first place that attracted my attention and I visited, was King Jimmy's Well. Here I fell in with bad company consisting of three low blackguard 'prentice lads from the Close. Having no wish to have any thing to say to them, I endeavoured to shun their company – but they, seeing me in a strange and perhaps somewhat clownish dress, followed and insulted me, and this they persisted in 'till I could bear it no longer, when turning upon one of the sauciest of them, I presently levelled him and was about serving the second in the same way, when they all three fell upon me and shewed no mercy, so that in the end I went home to my master's house with a scratched face and black eyes. This was an abominable sight to the family which no excuse could palliate. After this I was obliged to attend my master to church twice a day (forenoon and afternoon) every Sunday, and at night to read the Bible or some other good book, to old Mrs Beilby and her daughter, or others of the family – and this continued during the time of the term I boarded in the house with them. The father of this family followed the business of a gold-smith and jeweller, in Durham, where he had been greatly respected. He had taken care to give all his family a good education. His eldest son, Richard, had served his apprenticeship to a die sinker or seal engraver in Birmingham; his second son William had also learned enamelling and painting in the same place. The former of these had taught my master Ralph seal cutting and the latter taught their brother Thomas and sister Mary, enamelling and painting – and in this way this most industrious and respectable family lived together and maintained themselves. But prior to this state of things, while the family were more dependant upon the industry of their father, he failed in business, left Durham and

[60]

begun business in Gateshead, where he, as well as his eldest son Richard, died.

I was informed that about this period the family had to struggle with great difficulties, and that by way of helping to get through them, their mother taught a school in Gateshead; but this state of things could not last long, for the industry, ingenuity and the united energies of the family, must soon have enabled them to soar above every obstacle. My master had wrought as a jeweller with his father, before he went to his brother Richard to learn seal cutting, which was only for a very short time before his death. He also assisted his brothers and sister, in the constant employment of enamel painting upon glass.

At this time a fortunate circumstance, for my future master happened, which made an opening for him to get forward in his business unopposed by any one in Newcastle. An engraver of the name of Jameson, who had the whole stroke of the business in Newcastle to himself, having been detected in committing a forgery upon the old Bank, was tried for the crime, but his life was saved by the perjury of a Mrs Gray, who was I believe transported for it, and Jameson left the town. For sometime after I entered to the business, I was employed in drawing Copeland's *Ornaments*, and this was the only kind of drawing upon which I ever had a lesson given to me from any one. I never was a pupil to any drawing master and had not even a lesson from William Beilby and his brother Thomas, who along with their other profession, were also drawing masters; and afterwards I never had any opportunity or time to spare for any such purpose, at which I felt much grieved and disappointed, for my master kept me otherwise fully employed. The first jobs I was put to do was blocking out the wood about the lines on the diagrams, which my master finished, for the *Ladies Diaries* on which he was employed by Charles Hutton,* and etching sword blades for William and Nicholas Oley, sword manufacturers etc at Shotley-bridge.

* Afterwards the great Dr Hutton – he died 27 January 1823 in the 86th year of his age.

It was not long 'till the whole of the *Diagrams* were wholly put into my hands to finish. After these I was kept closely employed upon a variety of other jobs, for such was the industry of my master that he refused nothing, coarse or fine. He undertook everything and did it in the best way he could. He fitted up and tempered his own tools, which he adapted to every purpose and learned me to do the same. This readiness to undertake, brought him in an overflow of work and our work place was filled with the coarsest kinds of steel stamps – pipe moulds – bottle moulds – brass clock faces – door plates – coffin plates – bookbinders' letters and stamps – steel, silver and gold seals – mourning rings – arms, crests and cyphers on silver and every kind of job from the silver smiths – writing engraving of bills, bank notes, bills of parcels, shop bills and cards – these last, with gentlemen's arms for their books, he executed as well as most of the engravers of the time – but what he most excelled in was ornamental silver engraving: in this, as far as I am able to judge he was one of the first in the kingdom – and I think upon the whole, he might be called 'an ingeneous self taught artist'. The higher department of engraving such as landscape or historical plates, I dare say was hardly ever thought of by my master, at least not till I was nearly out of my apprenticeship, when he took it into his head to leave me in charge of the business at home, and of going to London, for the purpose of taking lessons in etching and engraving and practising upon large copper-plates. There was however little or no employment in this way in Newcastle, and he had no opportunity of becoming clever at it, so he kept labouring on with such work, as before named, in which I aided him with all my might. I think he was the best master in the world for

[62]

learning boys, for he obliged them to put their hands to every variety of work – every job, coarse or fine, either in cutting or engraving, I did as well as I could, cheerfully, but the wearisome business of polishing copper plates and hardning and polishing steel seals, was always irksome to me. I had wrought at such as this a long time, and at the coarser kind of engraving, (such as I have noticed before) 'till my hands became as hard and enlarged as those of a blacksmith. I however in due time, had a greater share of better and nicer work given me to execute – such as the outside and inside mottos on rings – and sometimes arms and crests on silver, and seals of various kinds, for which I made all the new steel punches and letters. We had a great deal of seal cutting, in which my master was accounted clever and in this I did my utmost to surpass him. While we were going on in this way, we were occasionally applied to by printers to execute wood cuts for them. In this branch my master was very defective; what he did was wretched and he did not like it – on which account such jobs were given to me, and the opportunity this afforded me of drawing the designs on the wood, was highly gratifying to me. It happened that one of these, a cut of the 'George and Dragon', for a barr bill, attracted so much notice and had so many praises bestowed upon it, that this kind of work greatly increased upon us, and were followed by cuts for children's books, chiefly for Thomas Saint, the Newcastle printer and successor of John White, who had rendered himself famous for his numerous publications of histories and old ballads. With the singing of the latter, the streets of Newcastle were long greatly enlivened, and many market day visitors, as well as the town's people, were often highly gratified. What a chearful lively time this appeared to me and many others. This state of things however, in time was changed, when public matters cast a surly gloom over the character of the whole country and these singing days, instead of being regulated by the magistrates, were, in their wisdom, totally put an end to.

My time now became greatly taken up with wood cutting a set of designs in that way, for 'the Storey Teller' – 'Gay's Fables' and 'the Select Fables' etc, together with cuts of various and of similar kinds for other printers. Some of the fables cuts were thought so well of by my master, that he in my name sent impressions of a few of them to be laid before the Society for the Encouragement of Arts etc, and I obtained a premium. This I received shortly after I was out of my apprenticeship and it was left to my choice whether I would have it in a gold medal or in money – £7.7s. I preferred the latter, and I never in my life felt greater pleasure than in that of presenting it to my mother. On this occasion, among the several congratulations of kind neighbours, those from Mr

[63]

Gregson, my old school master, stood preeminent – he flew from Ovingham, where the news first arrived – over to Eltringham to congratulate my father and mother upon the occasion, and the feelings and overflowings of his heart – can be better imagined than described.

5

During the time I was an inmate in my master's house, along with his
mother, brothers and sister, I attended his brother's horse and made
myself as useful to the family as I could. At that time I had no
acquaintances, at least none to be very intimate with. I neaded none – I
wandered in the fields and on the Town Moor alone, and amused
myself with my own thoughts. When the time arrived that I was to cater
for myself, upon 4/6d and afterwards upon 5s per week, I went to lodge
with my Aunt Blackett in the Pudding Chare, and she, being a Free-
man's widow,* kept cows upon the Moor and I was abundantly
supplied with milk, which was the chief thing I lived upon.

At this place I first got acquainted with Gilbert Gray the bookbinder,
and this remarkable, singular and worthy man, was the most valuable
(perhaps the most invaluable) acquaintance and friend I ever met with.
His moral lectures and advise to me, was a most important succedanium
to those imparted by my parents. His wise remarks – his detestation of
vice – his industry and his temperance, crowned with a most lively and
cheerfull disposition – altogether ever through life made him appear to
me as one of the best characters of the age. In his work shop I often
spent my winter's evenings, and this was also the case with a number of
other young men, who might be considered as his pupils – many of
whom (I have no doubt) he directed into the paths of truth and
integrity, and who *revered* his memory thro' life. He rose early to work,
he lay down when he felt weary, and rose again to it, when refreshed.
His diet was of the most simple kind, and of this he eat when hungry
and drank when dry, without paying regard to meal times. By steadily
pursuing this mode of life he was enabled to accumulate sums of money
from ten to thirty pounds; this enabled him to get books of an entertaining and of a moral tendancy, printed and circulated at a cheap rate. His
great object was, by every possible means, to promote honourable
feelings in the minds of youth and to prepare them for becoming good
members of society. I have often discovered that he did not overlook
ingenious mechanics, whose misfortunes, perhaps mismanagement,
had led them to a lodging in Newgate – to these he directed his compassionate eye, and to the deserving (in his estimation) he paid the

* of Thomas Blackett, Silversmith. This man, who was one of my godfathers, had been
foreman to the late John Langlands, where he was much noticed as a man of a most
intrepid spirit and rendered remarkable for his honour, honesty and punctuality.

debt and set them at liberty. He felt hurt at seeing the hands of an ingenious man tied up in a prison, where they were of no use, either to themselves or to the community. This worthy man had been educated for a priest, but he would say to me 'of a trouth, Thomas, I did not like their ways', so he gave up the thoughts of being a priest, and bent his way from Aberdeen to Edinburgh, where he engaged himself to Allan Ramsay the poet, then a bookseller in the latter place, and in whose service he was both a shopman and bookbinder. From Edinburgh he came to Newcastle and engaged himself, I believe, to Mr Slack as a bookbinder and as a faithfull and carefull inspector of the books printed in that office. Mrs Slack, who was a woman of uncommon abilities and great goodness of heart, did not overlook Gilbert and he was her *right hand man* as long as she lived. He was afterwards employed in the same way to the end of his life, under Solomon Hodgson, the successor to Thomas Slack.

Gilbert had had a liberal education bestowed upon him, had read a great deal, and reflected upon what he had read; this, with his retentive memory, enabled him to be a pleasant and communicative man – but something of a prejudice against priests stuck by him as long as he lived. I lived in habits of intimacy with him to the end of his life, and when he died, I with others of his friends attended his remains to the grave – at the Ballast Hills. He died on the 12 February 1794, in the 86th year of his age. I think his age was not known – some people said he was 84 while others called him 90.

In my attendance at the workshop of Gilbert, I got acquainted with several young men who like myself admired him – but one of the most singular of these, was Anthony Taylor, a glass maker. He was a keen admirer of drawings and paintings, but had no opportunity of shewing his talents in the arts, otherwise than in his paintings and his enamelling upon glass, in which way, considering his situation, he was a proficient; and in other respects he was a man of genious and observation. But the first interview I had with him was singular enough and was owing to his having been told, that I was the best whistler in England – he himself being remarkable in this way. We soon tried our respective powers and had many a meeting afterwards for that purpose. He expressed himself highly pleased with the loud and powerfull way in which I performed my double whistle, and I was equally so at hearing his inimitable shakes and quavers with which his small shrill *pipe* was graced. I came nearly up to the loud shrill tones of the fife and the deeper ones of the flute and improved greatly in imitating him, but he could make no alteration or amendment in his manner of performing and with all his attempts could

[66]

never whistle louder or deeper than before. We sometimes amused ourselves, turn and turn about, in this way and both agreed that it was a great pity that whistling was not more countenanced and encouraged than it was. We kept up an agreeable intimacy for some years untill he went to the glass works at Leith – where he ended his days. While I remained at my Aunt Blackett's, she never would allow me to whistle in her house or to try to perform upon any musical instrument, and I could not afterwards find either time or opportunity to gratify my propensity in this way, so I was obliged to make whistling serve for all. I often think it was scarcely possible for any one to have a better ear for music than I

had, for what ever tunes I heard at fairs or hoppings etc, I could next morning whistle them correctly, and not only the tune, but the manner of the various performers. I have ever since that time, been more and more confirmed in this opinion, and think it is not at all known to what pitch of perfection this most agreable species of music might attain to, were it encouraged. It would, I have no doubt, be found to surpass, in natural sweetness, any wind instrument whatever. To set it agoing would only require the aid of a few amateurs, who by forming themselves into something like a managing committee in every village where fairs or hoppings are held – and by collecting a small subscription from the performers and from others a more liberal sum – could award the money thus raised, to those who excelled in this way and who surpassed their competitors. There can be little doubt that contests of this agreable kind, would be found to throng the place and give a new character of cheerfulness to these meetings.

I think, were whistling encouraged at the theatre, from its novelty, it would draw together fuller meetings than is too often met with there, and empty seats would not be quite so common.

How long I lodged with my aunt, I have now forgot. After I left her

[67]

house I went to lodge with Ned Hatfield, whose wife was an excellent cook and market woman, and had long lived in the family of 'Willy Scott', the father of the present Lord Chancellor of England. She was now chiefly employed in keeping the dancing school of Neil Stewart, clean and in good order, and sold oranges and fruit etc to his pupils – above the school she had the rooms taken to live in and to let out to lodgers, and it happened that the young man, John McDonald, Mr Stewart's fidler, was lodged with her along with me – he was accounted an excellent performer on the violin* and to his performances (the Scottish tunes particularly) I listned with great delight. When Neil Stewart declined, or perhaps died, he was succeeded in this school by Ivey Gregg, and his fidler John Frazier lodged in the same house with me, and with his music I was also pleased as I had been before.

After this, my landlord got into a very unfortunate way of doing business, for being a heckler (flax dresser), his brethren prevailed upon

him and his wife to permit the tramps or *scamps*, in that line, to take up their lodgings with them. Here I was introduced to, or at least had an opportunity of becoming acquainted with them – *and a pretty set* they were – their conduct was wicked in the extreme. It had however the proper effect upon me, for I looked upon their behaviour with the utmost disgust. After poor Ned had for sometime been cheated and defrauded by this set, he at length got done with them and boarded and lodged others of a better *cast of character*. Long before the death of my friend Gilbert, I had not the same opportunities of getting or of reading his books, and what I could save out of my wages, could only afford me a scanty supply in this way. I had however an opportunity by favor of my master's servant girl, who admitted me early in the morning into his parlour, of reading through with great attention, the new publication of Smollet's *History of England* – for a long time afterwards I clearly remembered every thing of note, it contained. With some of the characters which he depictured I was greatly pleased, but with others, for the most part I was shocked and disgusted, for they appeared to me

* He afterwards was a dancing master of eminence at Perth in Scotland, where he died.

[68]

like fiends obtruded upon society – as a curse and a scourge to Mankind – and yet how surprizing it is that some of these can be spoken of, by authors, with complacency. Another source of my getting a supply of information, presently fell in my way through the kindness of William Gray,* the son of Gilbert, whose work shop now became a place of resort to me and to others. He was a bookbinder of repute and this led him into employment of a superior cast to that of his father, and his workshop was often filled with the works of the best authors, to bind for gentlemen. To these, while binding, I had ready access – for which purpose I rose early in the morning; and to him, my well known whistling in the street, was the signal for his quickly preparing to get to his work, and there I remained with him 'till my work hour came.

I feel it a misfortune that a bias somehow or other, took place in my mind at this time, and led me deeply into the chaos of what is called Religious Works, and for the purpose of getting into a thorough knowledge of all matters of this important kind, I spent much time, and took great pains and labour to obtain information, but instead of which I got myself into a labyrinth, bewildered with dogmas, creeds and opinions – mostly the finatical reveries of bigotted, or the inventions of interested or designing men, that seemed to me to be without end, and after all my pains I left off in a more unsettled state of mind than when I begun. I may be mistaken, but I think many a well meaning man has spun out his life and spent his time on subjects of this kind, in vain, and waggon loads of sermons have been published and have disappeared – some of them perhaps good – while others have been labouring to prove

* William Gray was a most active and industrious man; of an ardent but changeable temper. He began business in Newcastle, and prospered – he went to London and did the same – he returned to Newcastle, and to the binding business he added that of bookseller. On this occasion Jonathan Kidd and myself became bound for him for £60 – for the payment of which, his goods and books were left to us to sell. In this *freak*, for he had no occasion to fail, he wrote to me begging I would send him the books and goods, and knowing his integrity, I got my fellow bondman (with a good deal of trouble) to assent to this proposal and the books were sent off to him. He commenced auctioneer and soon paid us every penny of the money. He afterwards begun business in Nottingham as booktrader, printer and stationer, and there he failed – he continued his auctioneering from place to place for some time – and at length became a soldier – in this, his energy and activity became so conspicuous that he was employd as an inspector (I believe) of some of the military hospitals in Ireland – and had a pension settled upon him. He afterwards commenced the business of bookseller, bookbinder etc at Stonehouse, Plymouth – and at the same time followed that of auctioneering. At length however he took entirely to auctioneering and that of the shop was turned over to his son, who knew better than his father had done to conduct himself steadily.

[69]

matters (in my opinion) of no kind of use or importance either to religion or morality. If it be true that every thing in perfection is simple, so it will be with religion, as well as with other things. In this case there may be many moral and religious duties for Man to fulfill in his passage through life, but the rules for doing so are so plain and easily understood that commonsense only is necessary for all that is required of us. The beauty and simplicity of the doctrines laid down by the inspired and benevolent Author of the Christian Religion, however they may have

been distorted and disfigured, are yet in themselves perfect – they may indeed be compared to a mathematical point – a point of perfection – for all men to aim at, but which they cannot fully attain. The inspired writings of the prophets of old, are also full of simplicity as well as of indescribeable beauty, and may be read and considered without the fear of being tired of them. The inspired writers, poets and moralists, of more modern times have also laboured and most clearly so, to point out the paths which lead to virtue, to religion and to happiness. After all this, as far as I am able to judge of these matters, all we can do is to commune with and to reverence and adore the Creator, to yeild with humility and resignation to His will. With the most serious intention of forming a right judgement on this business, all the conclusion I can come to, is that there is only one God and one religion, and I know of no way so well of what is called serving God, as that of being good to his creatures, and of fulfilling the moral duties, as that of being good sons, brothers, husbands, fathers, neighbours and members of society.

About this time, I had few that I could call intimate acquaintances, my almost only ones were books, over which I spent my time, mornings and evenings, late and early. This too intense application to books together with my sedentary employment, and being placed at a very low work bench, took away my healthy appearance, and I put on a more delicate look. After being some time in this way, I became poorly in health, and when my master saw this, he sent for medical aid and Nathanial Bailes,* surgeon, was consulted – but before he uttered a word as to my ailment, he took me to his own house and there he stripped and examined me, and then, looking me in the face, told me I was as 'strong as a horse' – he then made up some slight medicine to cause me to spit up some phleghm which was gathering in the glands of the gullet or throat. This was all soon done, but not so with the lectures he gave my master, whom he addressed in terms which I thought both long and rude. 'What!' said he, 'and have you no more sense than to set a growing country lad to work, doubled up at a low bench, which would inevitably destroy him?' and in his passion, he cursed poor Beilby for his ignorance – or for something worse.

From this time the doctor took a liking to me and often criticised the work which I had executed. He also took great pains to direct me how to live and manage myself, under so sedentary an employment, and an intimacy took place between us, which lasted as long as he lived. He urged upon me the necessity of temperance and exercise. I then begun to act upon this advise and to live as he directed, both as to diet and

---

* He was commonly called Dr Bailes. He was a Newcastle worthy and accounted a man of great skill in his profession; he was also eminent for his learning and other attainments, and he was also called 'the eloquent Sword Bearer'. He headed the committee of the Burgesses in 17[73] who tried and beat the Magistrates respecting their exclusive claim to the Town Moor and was active in every thing relative to the good of the town. He was of an ingenious and enterprizing mind – a tolerably good engraver and a good mechanic. He invented a harpoon for killing whales, for which he got a patent – this was the most dreadfull instrument I ever saw: it was of a triangular shape and looked like 3 razors, back to back and brought to a sharp point and strongly barbed at their termination towards the socket. If this instrument was thrown so as to fall flat upon the back of a whale – the two undermost barbs were sure to lay hold of the skin and enter deeper and deeper – but if the animal was struck with the point of the instrument, it was sure to bury itself, shaft and all, overhead in the whale and could not be pulled out, without making a large hole, even into the crang or fleshy part – and thus wounded, the whale soon died and the usual lines and cords were nearly all saved. His charge for the harpoons was 3 guineas each – this price was deemed too high and was the cause of a confedracy of harpoon makers, sea captains and others, who knew not how to appreciate their value, to set their faces against using them. The 'Doctor', who did not like to be kept debating with ignorance and prejudice, and not being actuated by pecuniary motives, suffered the business to go to neglect. He died after being cut for the stone by Dr Ingham, 16 July 1791 aged 74 and was buried in St Nicholas's Church.

[71]

exercise. I had read Lewis Cornaro and other books which treated of temperance, and I greatly valued the advise in the *Spectator*, which strongly recommended all people to have their days of abstinence. In this, thro' life, I have experienced the uncommon benefits derived from occasionally pursuing that plan – for this always kept the stomach in a proper tone. I regularly pursued my walks and while thus exercising, my mind was commonly engaged in considering upon plans about how I should conduct myself in life, and of forming resolutions on such as I approved of, and of strictly acting up to them. For a long time, in both summer and winter, I mostly went to Elswick, three times a day, at the expence of a penny each time, for bread and milk. I had an hour allowed for my dinner time, and as to my mornings and evenings, I could take a much longer time. A very small matter of animal food, when I missed going to Elswick, was amply sufficient for me, for I think my constitution was of that kind which did not require to be stimulated. By persevering in this system of temperance and exercise, I was astonished to find how much I improved in health strength and agility. I thought nothing of leaving Newcastle (occasionally) after I had done work (7 o'clock) in a winter's night and of setting off to walk to Cherryburn – in this I was stimulated by an ardent desire to visit my parents as often as possible, and this desire continued to act upon me as long as they lived. In my solitary walks (as before noticed) the first resolution I recollect of having made, was that of living within my income, and another, of similar import, was that of never getting any thing upon trust. My limited income, indeed, led me carefully to observe these rules, but I never afterwards forgot them. The train of reflections they brought along with them, have also dwelt upon my mind. I could not help observing the inevitable ill consequences which a contrary course, at first perhaps unthinkingly, led thousands into, and the misery which it entailed. The more I have thought upon this subject through life, the more clearly do I see the importance of it – for getting into debt, is followed by leading on people to live bejond their income – and this makes all who do so, soon become demoralised and dishonest, and when the mind has been thus blunted and degraded, anxiety and trouble must be its attendants, 'till vice and misery close the scene. Among the acquaintances I made at the work shop of Gilbert and William Gray, was William Bulmer, afterwards rendered famous as the proprietor of the Shakspere Printing Office in Cleveland Row and who was the first that set the example and soon led the way to fine printing in England. He used, while he was an apprentice, to prove the cuts, I had executed – in this he was countenanced by his master, John Thompson Esqr who

[72]

was himself extremely curious and eager to see this succeed; but at that time, the printing of wood cuts properly, was very imperfectly known. About the same time, I commenced a most intimate acquaintance and friendship with Robert Pollard, afterwards an engraver and printseller of eminence in London. He was bound apprentice to John Kirkup, a silversmith, in Newcastle, and from his being frequently sent to our work place with crests, cyphers etc to engrave, he took a great liking to engraving and was indefatigable in his endeavours to become master of it. In furtherance of this, we spent many of our evenings together in his father's house, which to me was a kind of home. On his master Kirkup's declining business, my young friend was engaged for a term of years, to learn engraving with Isaac Taylor of Holborn, London.

In my frequent visits to the work shops of Gilbert Gray or to his son William's, I first fell in with Thomas Spence,* and afterwards became very intimate with him. He was one of the warmest philanthropists in the world – the happiness of mankind, seemed with him to absorb every other consideration; he was of a most cheerful disposition, warm in his attachments to his friends and in his patriotism to his country – but was violent against people, who he considered to be of an opposite character – with such he kept no bounds. For the purpose, chiefly I believe, of making converts to his way of thinking about 'property in land being

* Rendered, afterwards, famous in London as being at the head of the *Spenceans*, and sent to Dorchester Gaol for (I believe) some of his publications, for promulgating his doctrines in that way. He taught a school in the Broad-garth, Newcastle – afterwards taught writing and arithmetic etc in the great school at Haydon Bridge and lastly he was master of St Ann's public school in Sandgate. At this time his wife kept a shop at the Black Gate, and by her mismanagement, Spence (who was a carefull sober man) failed and was led into great difficulties – on which account he gave up St Ann's School, and went to London. Sometime before this, he was a member of a most respectable literary and philosophical society in Newcastle – one of their rules required that each member should read in turn a written lecture on any subject he pleased – Spence's was of course on that of 'property in land' etc. These lectures of the members, was by them prohibitted from publication; this rule Spence broke through by publishing his lecture, on which account he was expelled.

[73]

every one's right' – he got a number of young men gathered together and formed into a debating society, which was held in the evenings, at his first school room, in the Broad-garth, Newcastle. One night, when his favourite question was to be debated, he reckoned upon me as one of his *backers*. In this however he was mistaken, for notwithstanding my tacitly assenting in a certain degree to his plan, viz. as to the probable eligeability of its succeeding in some uninhabited country or island, yet I could not at all agree with him in thinking it right to upset the present state of society, by taking from people what was their own and then to launch out upon his speculations – for I considered that property ought to be held sacred, and besides, I considered the honestly obtaining [of] it, was the great stimulant to industry, which keeps all things in order, and society in full health and vigour. The question being given against him, without my having said a word in its defence, he became swollen with indignation which, after all the company were gone, he vented upon me; to reason with him was useless – he began by calling me (from my silence) a Sir Walter Blackett, and adding 'if I had been as stout as you are I would have thrashed you' – 'indeed!' said I 'it is a great pity you are not' – 'but' said he, 'there is another way in which I can do the business, and have at you!' – he then produced a pair of cudgels – and to work we fell. He did not know that I was a proficient in this art – and I soon saw he was very defective. After I had black'ned the insides of his thighs and arms, he became quite outrageous, and behaved very unfairly, which obliged me to give him a severe beating. This however did not make a breach between us, for I believe the respect and kindness for each other was mutual. I cut the steel punches, for his new types and my master struck them into the matrixes for casting his newly invented letters of the alphabet for his spelling and pronouncing dictionary. He published many curious books, in the same way of spelling, in London, and I believe all or most of them on this favourite subject of his, about 'Property in land being every one's right'. However mistaken he might be in his notions on this subject, yet I am clear in opinion his intentions were both sincere and honest.

The next most singular, or excentric, and at the same time one of the most worthy characters, I early got acquainted with was George Gray, the son of Gilbert, and half brother to William Gray. He was bound apprentice to a man of the name of Jones, a fruit painter; this man who I believe was accounted eminent in his profession, lived beyond his income and departed from Newcastle. George being thus left to himself, commenced in the same way of business, greatly succeeded in it, and then also became eminent as a fruit painter. This he pursued many years, but from his versatility of disposition, he dipped into almost every art and science, and became of first rate estimation in many of them. He was accounted one of the best of botanists and chemists in this country; he was also a geologist, and was fixed upon as a leader or director to a party, employed by Prince Poniatowsky, to take a survey of the various strata of Poland, but George, from the slovenly appearance of his dress – in which he was very negligent – felt himself slighted, and left those who put on a more respectable appearance, to profit by his

superiour knowledge to do the best they could, and he returned home. Whether it was before or after this time, I have forgot, but he paid a visit to North America and travelled in quest of knowledge pretty far back into the interiour of that country. He returned home to his old employ-ment and there in a room never cleaned nor swept out, he pursued his business – surrounded with models, crucibles, gallow pots, brushes and paints, pallets, bottles, jars, retorts and distills – in such a chaos of con-fusion as no words can describe. From this Sanctum Sanctorum, he corresponded with gentlemen of science in London and other parts. Few men were better liked by several private friends of this character – as well for his knowledge as for his honesty and the genuine simplicity of his manners. He died on the 9th of December 1819 aged 61 years, and was buried in St John's Church yard.

In addition to the various jobs already noticed as keeping my master and myself so fully employed – I had others which fell exclusively to my lot to execute, and these were the mathematical figures for Charles

Hutton. This frequently drew him into the room in which I worked, to inspect what I was doing. He was always very civil but seemed to me to be of a very grave or shy deportment. He lived in habits of intimacy with my master, and at that time used occasionally to write pieces for him to engrave from, but particularly for the heads of invoices, or bills of parcels – and I remember well his writing them with an ink or preparation which was easily transferred to the copper. This was before his appointment in the Royal Military Academy of Woolwich in 1773, and long before he had the well merited title of LLD added to his respected name. Dr Hutton was that kind of man who never forgot his old friends and some years after this, when I was in partnership with my old master, he recommended us to the notice of Dr Horsley,* who was commencing his publication of the whole of Sir Isaac Newton's Works. Materials were furnished us, on which to give an estimate of the expense of the whole. For this purpose, my partner first took this business into consideration, and when done, it next became my turn to estimate, and when we were both done, these were compared and the difference being trifling, a line was drawn between them and sent to Dr Hutton, and our charge was quite agreed to – when without delay, the figures were begun upon; and being now quite expert at this kind of work, the execution of the whole devolved upon me. This transaction took place in the [year] 1778.

But before this period, I still continued to take up my abode with Ned Hatfield and the spirits being bouyant, every thing pleased me. I cannot help noticing the happy time I spent with him. I was also entertained with the curious characters who resorted to his house – these were mostly bird catchers and bird dealers, with whose narratives respecting their pursuits, I listened to with some interest while they were enjoying themselves over a tankard of beer. Ned was almost constantly busied in rearing a very numerous brood of canaries, which he sold to a bird merchant who travelled with them at set times to Edinburgh, Glasgow etc for sale. I also at various periods of the time I remained under his roof, got fully into a knowledge of the misguided ways which too many young fellows pursued, and I watched and saw the wretched consequences of the kind of life they led. The first of these was a young man from the country of a hale healthy look and also of a good disposition, whose friends had it in their power and intended to enable him to prosper in the world, but he was chopped down in his *youthfull prime* solely by his connecting himself with the bad women of the town and becoming perfectly tainted by his intercourse with them.

* Afterward Bishop of St Asaph.

Two others, his companions, the same as to health, vigour and prospects in life as himself, fell sacrifices in the same way. I felt grieved for them and did all in my power to dissuade them from pursuing such a wretched course of life – for this advice they laughed at me and called me 'the old man'. It was not very long, however, after this 'till two of them sent for me to come and see them – *on their death beds*. The die was then cast, and I cannot forget their thanks to me and the bitterness with which they reproached themselves for not listening to what I had so sincerely recommended. Doctors may palliate this odious disease, thus contracted, and some may think in certain stages of it that it can be routed out of the habit – but this I think is doubtfull – and under this

impression I think that men so patched up, ought never to be allowed to marry, for [fear of] a tainted innocent offspring, and an endless train of diseases, which must continue to puzzel medical men, and mostly appear in one shape or other to hang upon them for life. Another young fellow (and I am done with them) whose prospects in life was as fair as those I have described, but whose character was of the basest kind, had led a similar course of life, and had got the disease patched up, and shocking to relate, he married – yes he married – as healthy, beautiful and innocent [a] young woman as could be seen – with a fortune too. Well in due time there appeared a prospect of his becoming a father. The time came – but it is too shocking and disgusting to relate further particulars. Shortly after this, he married another young woman of a similar description as the last, and a similar wretched fate attended her – for a great length of time after this I lost sight of him, but by chance fell in with him again, when he accosted me with all the familiarity of an old acquaintance and fellow lodger. I was so overpowered with disgust that a civil return was out of my power to give him. 'So', said I, 'and is it you? I suppose you think, by your having turned Methodist you will rub off your enormous crimes – no, no, you may think that preaching and praying will wipe off the stain – but I think not,' and in the heat of my indignation, forgot myself and said, 'if I were God I never would forgive you. What God may do in his infinite mercy I know not.' He died in his prime a short time after this. Such conduct as I have been attempting to describe, appears to me to be of the very blackest die; it is amongst the most cruel and the most shocking of murders. It is to be regretted that the seducer and the seduced, cannot, by any known law, be obliged to live together for life, and while they lived, to be allowed to herd only with such as themselves – for they ought to be banished from the society of the modest and virtuous part of the community. I think it a great omission in parents and teachers, not to make unguarded youth fully apprized of the risques they run in towns, of getting acquainted with the lost and polluted women of this stamp – nothing can be so sure a guard against this vice, as that of making young men see it in its true light, to be disgusted at it. Magistrates, no doubt, have it in their power, in some degree to lessen this great evil, by preventing bad women from appearing in the streets of a town and perhaps in brothells – but I have often felt for magistrates on account of the great and gratuitous trouble they take and the difficulties they must have to encounter in their endeavours to keep the wicked within due bounds.

My last fellow lodgers and associates at Ned Hatfield's, before I was done with my apprenticeship, was John Hymers (or Hindmarsh) who had been a Sergeant in the Life Guards and had retired upon his pension – and Whitaker Shadforth, clock and watch maker and also a musician.* The latter was of a quite different character from those before noticed, but was wild enthusiastic and romantic. When he first came to lodge with us, he had a pale, pasty and unhealthy look, with his stomach quite out of order – for the amendment of which I began to prescribe for him, and for this purpose I ordered him to prepare a quantity of warm camomile tea and then to set himself to work in smoking several pipes of tobacco. The effect produced by these kept him up all night, but gave him a most thorough clensing, and in a little time he appeared with a ruddy complexion and in good health. I next put him upon the same way of living as that I practised myself, and in this he persevered untill he became strong and active. Among the many whims and fancies which we indulged in, one of them was to learn the

* He left England and went to America before the war broke out between the two countries, and when this happened, he was obliged to serve in the American Army.

manual exercise. The Sergeant, who had often laughed at our frolics, very readily agreed to undertake this task, provided we would stricktly obey the rules he prescribed to us. This we agreed to. He begun a kind of lecture upon the necessity of soldiers being obedient to their officers and to stand like a brick wall without flinching, adding that he would not use his cane upon our backs but only to put us in mind that we should be very attentive. This being settled, we were in the mornings to appear before him in *bare buff*, that is without our shirts and upper clothing; this discipline we pursued steadily for sometime, notwith-standing the switches he gave us on our bare backs with his rod or cane – which we both bore with the utmost *sang froid*. I think the Serjeant, notwithstanding the entertainment we thus afforded him, begun to tire first, for he at last lay in bed while he was giving us our lessons, and at length gave the business up.

From the length of time I had known and noticed Miss Beilby, I had formed a strong attachment to her, but could not make this known either to her or to any one else. I would have married her before I was done with my apprenticeship, without any fears on my part; but I felt for her and pined and fretted at so many barrs being in the way against any union of this kind – one of the greatest was the supposed contempt in which I was held by the rest of the family, who I thought treated me with great hateur, 'tho I had done every thing in my power to oblige them. I had like a stable boy waited upon their horse and had cheerfully done every thing they wanted at my hands – 'till one of the brothers grossly affronted me in the business of the stable. This I instantly resented and refused attendance there any more. Before I was out of my time, Miss Beilby had a paralitic or palsy stroke, which very greatly altered her look and rendered her for sometime unhappy; she [not] long after this went with her eldest brother into Fifeshire where she died.

6

The first of October 1774 arrived at last and for the first time in my life I felt myself at liberty. I wrought a few weeks with my old master and then set off to spend the winter at Cherryburn. There I had plenty of work to do, chiefly from my friend Thomas Angus, the printer in Newcastle. I continued there, employed by him and others, and when wanted, by my old master, 'till the summer of 1776. This was a time of great enjoyment, for the charms of the country was highly relished by me, and after so long an almost abscence from it, gave even that relish a zest, which I have not words to express. I continued to follow wood cutting and other jobs, but often rambled about among old neighbours and became more and more attached to them as well as to my country. In the storms of winter (as before noticed) I joined the Nimrods of old – in spring and summer my favourite sport of angling, was pretty closely followed up. About Christmas, (as I had done before when a boy) I went with my father to a distance to collect the money due to him for his coals. In these rounds I had the opportunity of *seeing* the kindness and hospitality of the people – the countenances of all, both high and low, beamed with cheerfulness, and this was heightened every where, by the music of old tunes from the well known exhilerating wild notes of the Northumberland pipes, amidst the buz occasioned by various *foulploughs* (morrice or sword dancers) from various parts of the country. These altogether left an impression on my mind, *which the cares of the world* have never effaced from it. The gentry, the farmers and even the working people of that day, had their Christmas home brewed ale made only from malt and hops, before the pernicious use of chemical or druggists' compounds were known, or agricultural improvements had quickened the eyes of landlords, banished many small farmers, soured their countenances, and altered the characters for the worse of the larger ones that remained.

Having all my life, at home, at school and during my apprenticeship lived under perpetual restraints – when I thus felt myself at liberty, I became as I suppose, like a bird which had escaped from its cage. Even angling of which I was so fond, and of which I thought I never could tire, became rather dull when I found I might take as much of it as I pleased. While I was pursuing this sport, on a hot day in June, I gave it up and laying down my rod awhile, I then tied it up and walked home – having resolved to see more of the country. I requested my mother to put me up some shirts etc, and I told her I was going to see my uncle (her brother) in Cumberland. This was soon done amidst her expressions of fears for my safety, and shewing the natural feelings of a good mother. After sewing three guineas in my breeches waistband, I set off that afternoon and walked to Haydon-bridge. Here I visited my old crony Thomas Spence, (then a teacher in Haydon-bridge School) with whom I was a welcome guest, and with whom I stopped two days; and leave of abscence from school being given, I rambled with him over the neighbourhood and visited every thing worth notice. When I departed, he accompanied me on the road nearly to Haltwhistle. After this I met with little to attract notice except Naworth Castle, and when I left it and in proceeding across the country, I lost my way by following paths which led only to holes which had been made by digging peats and turf, and did not reach my uncle's house at Ainstable, till late in the evening. I remained at Ainstable about a week, in which time I rambled about the neighbourhood, visited my friends at Kirkoswald and elsewhere, and spent what time I could spare in fishing for trout in the Croglin; and after I had seen Armthwaite and Penrith, I began to think of moving farther abroad – and my cousin having occasion to go to Carlisle, I went with him there, where we parted. I wandered about the old city and in the afternoon looked into the shop of Lowrey the watchmaker, to whom I was only known so far as having been employed by my master [to] engrave many clock faces for him during my apprenticeship. While I was in his shop, in came a man – a *kind of scamp* – of the name of Graham, who asked me what road I was going. 'To Scotland' I replied – 'so am I' said he, and added, 'if you can keep foot with me, I will be glad of your company'. We had no sooner set off 'till I found he was one of those vapouring fops who was very proud of his great prowess as a pedestrian; I could soon see that he wanted to walk me *off my foot*, but [I] having been long trained or practised in this way, he felt himself mistaken, and long before we reached Longtown, he called in at several public houses for a refreshment and invited me to do the same. I however was not thirsty, and not being used to drink, I sat on the seats at the doors untill he came out. He kept on in this way 'till we reached Langholm, when he surveyed me with an attentive eye but said nothing. At Langholm, the landlord, who was a Cumberland man and knew my relatives there, was very kind to me, and among many other matters concerning them, he told me my cousin, who accompanied me to Carlisle, had won nine belts in his wrestling matches in that county. From Langholm I set off to Hawick and Selkirk, and from that place, next morning by Dalkeith to Edinburgh. I had been, in this short

[81]

tramp, particularly charmed with the Border scenery, the roads in places twined about the bottoms of the hills, which looked beautifully green like velvet, spotted over with the white sheep which grazed on their sides – watched by the peacefull shepherd and his dog. I could not help depicturing in my mind, the change of scenery which had taken place in these times, and comparing them with the times of old that had passed away, and in inwardly rejoicing at the happy reverse. It is horrid to contemplate upon the ferocious battles of that day between men descended from the same stock and bearing the same names, on both sides of the border, only divided from each other by a river, a rivulet, a burn or a stripe of ground – [that they] should be called out to the wild foray, by the slogan horn, or at the nod of their chieftains be gathered together, by the shrill notes of the bugle and led on to meet and slaughter each other – to manure the ground with their blood, amidst the clash of arms – and the thrilling music of their pipes which helped to exert them on to close their eyes in death. These transactions, which is handed down to their descendants of the present generation, in traditionary tales, and kept in remembrance by the songs and tunes of old times, serve only now as food for reflection or amusement.

On entering Edinburgh, having been recommended by Mr

Robertson, Silversmith, to the landlord of the George Inn, Bristoe Port, I halted there, but being quite unacquainted with the customs of living in such places, I knew not what to do, or how to conduct myself. I however called for a pint of beer, and I think it was the first I ever called for in my life, when lo! a good looking girl, bare footed and bare legged entered with a pewter pot almost the size of a half leg of a boot – this I thought I could not empty in a week. As I found I could not remain in this place, I sought about for another, and luckily fell in with an old Newcastle acquaintance Mrs Hales the wife (or widow) of Hales, the coachman to Lord Chief Baron Ord. To her I stated my case, went with her and felt quite at home in her house. After I had seen as much of *Auld Reeky* as I could, lost in admiration at the grandeur of its situation, and also the grandeur of its internal old buildings, I then next day called upon Hector Gavin, an engraver in Parliament Close. This kind man, a stranger to me, when after having had a bit of chat with him about the arts etc he threw by his tools and was quite at my service. The warmth of his kindness I never can forget – he took me all over Edinburgh and gave me a history and explanation of every thing he thought worthy of notice. Having parted with him with his best and warmest wishes, I rose early on the next morning and walked to Glasgow and after leaving my bundle at the inn there, to which Mr Robertson had also recommended me, I took a ramble through Glasgow. Here I fell in (by chance) with an old acquaintance Alexander Steedman, a clever cutler, who had lodged with me at Ned Hatfield's, and who I supposed was dead long ago. He was not like me, for he could drink plenty – so that I was at no loss what to do at the inn, as I had been in Edinburgh. He called upon me the next morning, along with a curious and well informed man, when they shewed me every thing they thought worth notice in Glasgow. I could see that Glasgow was a large city with many handsome buildings in it, but I was not so charmed with it as I had been with Edinburgh.

From Glasgow I set off to Dumbarton, and on my way took as good a survey of the country and whatever was new to me or curious, as I could. My landlord at Dumbarton had seen a deal of the world, either as a soldier or as a gentleman's servant, was very kind and communicative to me, and I think I spent the next day with him in walking about and viewing every thing that he could think of that might please or entertain me. After leaving him, I wished much to see the cotton works and the printing of it, at the printfields, as they were called, on the River Leven near Dumbarton. To these, however, I could not get admission, so I kept passing onward up the Leven, 'till Smollett's monument, near the side of it, arrested my attention. Here I stopped, for I had read Smollett's

[83]

Works and almost adored him as an author. On the pedestal of the monument was a long Latin inscription, which I was endeavouring to translate into English, but in this I was puzzled to make it out, having never looked into a Latin book since I left school, and this was the first time I felt mortified at having done so. While I was thus employed, up came a *leish* clever young man, a Highlander, smartly dressed in the garb of his country – he jumped down beside me and begun his translation, which we together made out. When this was done, on learning from me that my sole object was to see Scotland, he pressed me to accompany him to some place or other, the name [of] which I do not now remember. We however walked on the western side of Loch Lomond, a long way together, but I know I did not visit Inverary the Seat of Argyle – but stopt with him at a grazier's or farmer's house, perhaps not a long way from it. Having made up my mind not to visit any city or town, nor to put up at any inn, I commenced my *Wild Goose chase* and bent my way in many a zig zag direction through the interiour of part of the Highlands – by the sides of its lakes and its mountains. The beauty and serenity of the former and the grandeur or terrific aspect of the latter, I gazed upon with wonder, and with both was charmed to extacy. In moving forward I was often accompanied or directed to some farmer's or grazier's house, by the herds or drovers which I fell in with, and in some of these houses I took up my abode and often by the pressing solicitation of my host or hostess was prevailed upon to remain with them for a day or two. These kind, these hospitable people I never forgot. Often, the mistress of the house, in these remote places, never having seen any person from England, examined my dress from head to foot and in English which it was easy to discover, had been imperfectly taught her, made many enquiries respecting the country from whence I came, while the herds with their bare knees sat listning around, very seldom knowing what we were talking about. These herds, or some of the family, generally set or directed me to the house of some other distant grazier, where I met with the same kind and warm reception throughout my wanderings, as I had experienced at first. It sometimes happened that by my having stopped too long on my way in admiration of the varied prospects I met with, that I was benighted and was obliged to take shelter under some rockey projection, or to lay myself down among the heather 'till day light. In my traversings and wanderings, I called in at all the houses on my way, whether situated in the beautifull little vallies, watered by a brook, a burn or rivulet – or those in glens, or on the sides [of the] heathery hills. In these places, it was common to see three houses, one added to the end [of] another –

[84]

the first containing the young healthy looking children, of the last married couple – in the next or middle one was the father and mother and perhaps the brothers and sisters of this couple, and farther in, at the end, was the habitation of the old people, the grandfather and grandmother of the whole. These places had alway garths or gardens adjoining – with peat stacks and other fuel at hand for the winter, and the whole enlivened with numbers of duck, chickens etc. On my getting

some refreshment of whey or milk etc, in such like places as these, I always found it difficult to get payment made for any thing – as it seemed to give offence – and when I could get any money slipped into the hands of the children, I was sure to be pursued and obliged to accept of a pocket full of bannocks and scones. On one occasion, having been detained all day and all night at a house of this kind, in listning to the tunes of a young man of the family, who played well upon the Scottish pipes, and my having in turn whistled several Tyneside tunes to him, we could hardly get seperated. Before my departure next day, I contrived by stealth, to put some money into the hands of the children. I had not got far from the house 'till I was pursued by a beautifull young woman, who accosted me in *baddish* English, which she must have got off by *heart* just before she left the house, the purport of which was to urge my acceptance of the usual present. This I wished to refuse, but she pressed it upon me with such sweetness and with a face and neck blushed with scarlet, while I thought, at the same time she invited me to return – on which (I could not help it) I seized her and smacked her lips. She then sprung away from me, with her bare leggs, like a deer, and left me fixed to the spot, not knowing what to do. I was particularly

[85]

struck with her whole handsome appearance – it was a compound of loveliness, health and agility. Her hair I think had been flaxen or light, but was tanned to a pale sandy brown, by being exposed to the sun – this was tied behind with a ribbon and dangled down her back, and as she bounded along it flowed in the air. I had not seen her while I was in the house, and felt grieved because I did not hope ever to see her more.

After having wandered about in this way for sometime longer, in which I uniformly met with the same kind treatment, among these unpoluted, unspoiled, honourable and kind people, I began to think of the long way I had to get over on my return towards home, for although my money was not greatly diminished among the Highlanders, yet I knew not how much I might want in or near towns, in more *civilized* districts. So I turned back in a south easterly direction through the country, where I met, in my various windings among the same kind of people, the same warm and friendly reception. From that time to this, I have ever felt pleased at the name of Highlander. Were not these people proof against the bribe of thirty thousand pounds, held out to them to betray the unfortunate prince Charles Stewart? Have not *agricultural improvements* taught the landlords or chieftains, to whose forefathers they owed so much, to turn numerous farms into one? and by that means banished thousands of these hardy descendants of the ancient Britons – these brave race of men, to seek an assylum in foreign climes, and in exchange for whom, they have peopled the country with sheep. Property in every country ought to be held sacred, but it ought also to have its bounds, and (in my opinion) to be in a certain degree held in trust jointly for the benefit of its owners and the good of society of which they form a part. Bejond this is despotism, the offspring of misplaced aristocratic pride. I have not noticed that I was sometimes, in passing along, detained at fairs or trysts – these with their merry makings, were something like the hoppings and feasts on Tyne side and the girls had the same ruddy look as the farmers' servants who were put to do field work in

Northumberland and Durham. With the Scotch music and dancing I was very much pleased. They were certainly good dancers and seemed quite wild or exhilerated to excess.

I left this country with regret, and the last day's journey from it was a very long one, and a very hungry one, after which I was obliged to enter Stirling in the night. I told the landlord of the public house, that I was almost famished not having stopt at any house on my very long journey to that place, and begged of him to hasten to get me something to eat. He told me he had nothing left but eggs, for his company that day had eaten every thing that had been in [the] house quite up. I did not get my eggs 'till midnight, for a quarrel or an affray happened in the house at the time I ought to have had them. They were brought in to me at last and were boiled as hard as eggs could be – with them in my eagerness to eat I was nearly choaked. At Stirling I remained about two or three days, chiefly on account of my face having been so blistered by the heat of the sun, that I thought it best to halt 'till the effects of it could be removed. My landlord was very kind and was also one of those who had seen the world. When he found that I was an engraver, he expressed his surprize that I had not carried my tools with me, for if I had done so, he said he had no manner of doubt, with my knowledge of heraldry etc, that I could have found plenty of employment among the gentry and the lairds, in engraving their arms, crests and other devices – and [could] have earned easily far more than double the money of our Newcastle charges, besides being handed from chief to chieftain, and seeing the whole country in a very different way from that which I had, through wildernesses so wildly pursued. On my way to Edinburgh by Falkirk, I visited Carron Works and passed under the canal, where for the first time I saw vessels passing over my head. I was also shewn the ground where the Battle of Bannockburn was fought. As soon as I could, I made my way by Linlithgow to Edinburgh, and took up my abode again with Mrs Hales; and having engaged a passage by sea, in a ship belonging to Whitby which had to *touch* at Shields, I attended upon this vessel every tide, late and early, for several days – and at last I missed my time and was left behind. In this emergency I got on board a Leith sloop, bound for Newcastle, commanded by Captain Kay, then moving from the pier. We no sooner got down the Firth of Forth to the open sea than we met a very heavy swell, and presently was suddenly attacked by a violent gale which soon tore our *sails to shivers* and drove us far out of sight of land. This put our small crew in a great bustle and dilemma. In this small vessel the whole people and crew amounted to 26 – for these there

[87]

was no accomodation. The boat upon deck was full of the sick, covered by an old sail, and the rest were obliged to sit or to *lie* down in any corner where they could find a bit of room. The first night was a sickly suffocating one, and for three more, and three days (the length of our voyage to Shields) there was little or no amendment of our situation. On board this sloop there were only two beds that were not stowed with goods, and from my wanting rest so long before I left Edinburgh, I crept into one of them as soon as I could, but found it so low that I could not lie on my side, nor easily turn over, so I could get no sleep, and to mend the matter I had not been long in this wretched bed 'till a sucking infant was put in beside me, its mother being dismally sick in the boat upon deck – and the child fell exclusively into my charge. I nursed it as well as I could during the whole voyage and I think had I not done so it must have died. After resting a day or two at South Shields, I set off to Newcastle, where I arrived (in the Assize Week) I think on the 12 August 1776. After all my long abscence, I found I had a few shillings left. On this occasion my old friends in Newcastle quizzed me not a little, for having as they termed it, begged my way through Scotland.

7

I remained no longer in Newcastle than untill I earned as much money as would pay my way to London, and I then took my passage on board a collier bound to the great city; and after beating about in good weather and bad weather for about three weeks, we arrived in London on the 1st of October 1776. The first Cockney I met with was the scullar man, who was engaged to land me and my baggage at Carnegie's the hair dresser near Temple Barr. I was amused with his slang and his chatter all the way to London Bridge, and on his approaching it, he asked me if I was *affeared*, but not knowing what I was to be affraid of, I asked him the same question at which he looked *quere* – and in this way we passed the gulph, about which he wanted to talk, and I then asked him if he had been *affeard*. It was not long before I found out my old schoolfellows Christopher and Philip Gregson, and my old companion William Gray, now a bookbinder in Chancery Lane, and my old friend Robert Pollard. The first had provided me with a lodging, and the last, through the kindness and the influence of his master, Isaac Taylor, with plenty of work. Before I sat down to work, I thought it best to take a ramble through every part of both the city and its environs. The first day I went alone and saw nobody I knew; on the second day I fell in, by chance, with Serjeant Hymers, in the Strand – who on seeing me, seemed quite surprized. He held up both his hands – he looked – he laughed – shook me by the hand over and over again and seemed not to know how to be kind enough. He then took me back with him, 'till he got himself dressed, and when this was done, he made a very handsome appearance indeed. The rest of this day he wholly devoted to my service. He first took me to the blackguard places in London – I supposed this was with a view to corroborate the truth of the stories he had before told me in Newcastle. After I had seen enough of these places, he then took me to others of a more respectable character better worth notice. After rambling about afterwards with my warm friend the Serjeant, 'till I had seen a good deal of the interiour and the exteriour of London – of which it would be superfluous to give an account – I then sat down closely to work, untill I got through the wood cuts, which through Isaac Taylor's kindness had been provided for me. I then called upon Thomas Hodgson, printer in George's Court, Clerkenwell, who had also provided

* Thomas Hodgson had served his apprenticeship as a printer to John White of Newcastle (before named) and having taken a liking to wood ingraving, he employed

work for me, to meet my arrival in London, and who had waited impatiently for my assistance.*

Having served my time, as a kind of 'Jack of all trades', I felt desirous to work among the cockneys, to see if I could find any thing new among them, but in this I was disappointed – for I never could be permitted to see any of them at work. They indeed seemed desirous of seeing what I was doing, and occasionally peeped in upon me for that purpose, and I thought such of them as did so were a most saucy ignorant and impudent set. Where ever I went the ignorant part of the cockneys, called me 'Scotchman'. At this I was not offended, but when they added other impudent remarks, I could not stand them, and this often led me into quarrels such as I wished to avoid and had not been used to engage in. It is not worth while noticing these, but only as they served to help out my dislike to London – but this was only trivial compared with other matters. The first of these that struck me and what constantly hurt my feelings, was the seeing of such a number of fine looking women engaged in the wretched business of *Street Walking*. Of these, I often enquired as to the cause of their becoming so lost to themselves and to the world – their account of this, in their common replies, was that they had been seduced and then basely betrayed. This I believed,

and I was grieved to think that they were thus prevented from becoming perhaps the best of mothers to an offspring of lovely and healthy children. This I often told them and this ended in their tears; and if they were in poverty I contributed my mite to relieve them.

most of his time in embellishing the endless number printed at that office of the old ballads and histories, with rude devices as head-pieces to them. He was a most assiduous, carefull and recluse man. What he published in London, I cannot enumerate the number of, but I understood he employed some Germans as well as myself, to cut blocks for him; he also employed me to make designs for many of these cuts. When he died he left me a legacy of five pounds – and this was the first money I ever received that I had not wrought for.

What a pity this wretchedness is not prevented. Base men treat women as if they were inferiour beings made only to be used like brutes and tiranized over as their slaves. I have always beheld such conduct towards women with abhorrence, for my conceptions of this wretched state of things are of the most soul harrowing description. It would be extreme weakness to maintain an opinion that all women were good, and that the faults here noticed were always ascribeable to the men only – this is not the case, for I must be obliged to admit that there are good and bad of each sex. I have often attempted to make an estimate of their comparative numbers, in which I have felt some difficulties – sometimes my barometer of estimation has arisen to the height of ten to one in favour of the fair sex – at other times it has fluctuated and fallen down some degrees lower in the scale, but (with me), it is now settled, and I cannot go lower than four good women to one good man. I have often wondered how any man could look healthy beautifull, sensible and virtuous women in [the] face, without considering them as the link between men and angels; for my part I often felt my self so overpowered with reverence in their prescence that I have been almost unable to speak, and they must often have noticed my embarresment. I could mention the names of many but it might offend their delicacy. Where a *good* man can get such a help-mate for life, his happiness must be secured, for such a one is of inestimable value – 'her price is far above rubies'. On seeing such, and indeed others of the fair sex, I always inwardly thought, or muttered out – 'I cannot bless them – I would if I could – but may God bless them'.

In London one man does one branch of business and another another of the same kind of work, and it is by this division of labour they thus accomplish so much and so well. I however soon tired of thus working alone, and as I had plenty of work to do on my own account, from my former friends, to which were added Mr Carnan and Mr Newbery of St Paul's Church Yard – I turnd my back upon the masters who took in all kinds of work, and stuck to working for myself.

Having now been weaned from taking bread and milk, I had learned by degrees to call for a pint of porter, and often spent the evenings in 'The George', in Brook Street, kept by a person of the name of Darby – whose wife, a very good looking woman from Cumberland, claimed a distant relationship to me. At this house I often spent my evenings among some very respectable and pleasant tradesmen. While I was there one evening, a stranger to me joined with us, I think he was a traveller; he had however been in Scotland and had a mighty itch to speak very disrespectfully of that country and was vociforous in attempting to

entertain the company with his account of the filth and dirt he had met with in it. This I could not bear – their kindness was fresh in my memory and I felt resentment rising in me. I however quashed that feeling – and only told him that I believed I had travelled on foot, perhaps about 300 miles, through Scotland, and had met with no such people there, nor such dirtiness as he described. There might indeed be some such in every country, for ought I knew – but I was confident such might be found without going much bejond the street we were in, and who in addition to their filthiness, were also the most wretched and abandoned of the human race – some of them indeed appeared to me to be scarcly human. I concluded by observing that I was affraid he had been keeping very bad company in Scotland – a laugh by this, was raised against him and he felt himself quashed by his own folly. I very frequently visited Westminster Abbey, on some part of the Sunday, and on the forenoons of that day I mostly went with my friend Pollard to hear the Reverend Harrison at St Andrew's Church Holborn. I some-times also went to hear eminent preachers at other places. I was once invited by my friend William Watson of the Treasury (who had married the eldest Miss Beilby) to go with him to hear Dr Dodd preach, at the Magdalen Chappel, but whether this was at the time he was arrested for forgery or not, I am not certain, but I know I never saw him, nor heard him preach. I also went with Mr Watson to a place of this kind to hear the Reverend Maxwell another eminent divine, but indeed I believe I did not miss hearing any of the popular preachers in London. For many years after I left London, I still kept on in the same way and went

[92]

occasionally to hear the preachers of various persuasions, and attempted to find out the general character of their several congregations. Having been brought up under the creeds and doctrines of the Church of England, I *may* perhaps have some partialities about me respecting it, but I have ever considered that its clergy were the most learned of any, and that (excepting some of the higher orders of them) they were, as well as their hearers, the most tolerant. But I have ever felt greived that such a great number of them should consist of very learned and good men, with curacies or poor livings that did not afford them a much better income than the wages of common mechanics, and that however great their abilities might be, it was only by patronage that they could be advanced, while enormous stipends were lavished upon others, very often for the most useless, or perhaps the most corrupt purposes. I think it would be much better if their incomes could be equallized – but so long as matters are managed otherwise, so long will it be considered a system of revenue, of which religion is only the pretext. The Roman Catholic mode of faith is the oldest and they seem the most of any sect attached to it and its old customs and its old creeds, which they seem obstinately to value and persist in; and this most likely will continue, so long as they give up their own reason and implicitly obey that dictated to them by their priests. They are the strictist of all disiplinarians in their worship, and are also generally good members of society. The next, and most numerous sect, are the Methodists, and I fear if they had the upper hand they would soon shew a persecuting spirit, but which I hope will never more be suffered to rear its head. This sect took their rise under the able auspices of John Wesley, and at that time he did a great deal of good – in this neighbourhood it was soon made to appear, for he greatly civilized a numerous host of demi barbarians, the pitmen and others employed in the coal works; these seemed like tribes of Cherokees and Mohawks, but they were more wicked. What I have ever been able to discover of the general character of this sect is that a great number of them are ignorant bigotted fanatics. Before I left off going to hear them, it appeared clear to me that their discourses from the pulpit, were mostly unintelligible, and the more so this appeared to be, the more numerously were the congregations crouded together to hear such preachers and their jargon. There is another sect growing into great importance as a religious society and that is the Quakers – the 'Friends' as they properly denominate themselves. They have many excellent rules laid down by which to regulate their conduct in life, and with all their peculiarities, their simplicity of manners command the respect of the thinking part of mankind. They have, it

[93]

is true, been characterized as 'English Jews' by some, and others have said of them that they are not now a religious society, like the Methodists – 'they are an aristocratical civil community; a trading company, and a set of respectable, industrious economical, money getting disciplinarians; who possess no more practical religion than the members of the church of England'. This may no doubt be the opinion of some, but

I could never form such a one, of at least the great majority of them, for they appear to me to deserve a better character. I wish, indeed, to see them leave off a part of their puritanical appearance and some other stiffnesses in their deportment. Were all men Quakers, I think the world would have a very sombre appearance, but this is balanced by their keeping their word, by their detestation of war and by their constant endeavours to live in peace with all men. I have often wondered at their rejecting music. Music is an emanation from heaven – it is perfectly natural to man, to drive away gloom and to solace and to chear him. The beautifull choristers of the woods and the fields lead the way and set us the example.

The Unitarians are generally a well informed and respectable description of men – they think for themselves, and are not bewildered with dogmas and creeds. But to swell these opinions of mine with a further account of the peculiarities of each sect or, [to] attempt to go through the numerous descriptions of religionists, would be an endless and a dreary task. They ought each of them [to] be made wellcome to follow their own opinions, and I can only observe that if they are founded in truth, there can be no fear that they can be injured by

[94]

unreserved discussion, and whatever their creeds may be, there can be no objections to the religion of a virtuous man. It is hoped that this opinion will universally prevail, and that the distinctions and bickerings among different denominations of Christians will cease, and the causes of them be thought of no more importance than whether a man uses his quid of tobacco in the right cheek or in the left.

After this long digression I must now turn my attention again to London. My friend Mr Watson was very desirous to get me to work with Mr Pingo in the Mint, and from his being so well known and respected, by the gentlemen in most of the Government offices, he thought this might be easily accomplished. My mind was however bent quite another way, and no more was done for me in this business. The constant attention and kindness of my London friends, whose company I enjoyed, was unabated. They walked with me every where and the house of William Gray was a home to me. I met other Newcastle friends every Monday night at the Hole in the Wall, Fleet Street where I went to see the Newcastle papers. Some of these, indeed, occasionally wanted assistance and got my last sixpence. At this time I earned a deal of money, and from my habits of temperance I spent little for my own living, and thus for the first time, discovered what a small sum was sufficient to make me independant, and I never lost sight of the inestimable value of being so. I however, never had a surplus of cash long in my possession, for one or another had occasion for it – and I could not bear to see distress without relieving it. Notwithstanding my being so situated among my friends, and of being so much gratified in seeing such a variety of excellent performances in every art and science – painting, statuary, engraving, carving etc were to be seen every day,

[95]

yet I did not like London – it appeared to me to be a world of itself where every thing in the extreme, might at once be seen – extreme riches – extreme poverty – extreme grandeur and extreme wretchedness – all of which were such as I had not contemplated upon before. Perhaps I might indeed take too full a view of London on its gloomy side – I could not help it – I tired of it and determined to return home. The country of my old friends, the manners of the people of that day, the scenery of Tyne side, seemed altogether to form a paradise for me and I longed to see it again. While I was thus turning these matters over in my mind, my warm friend and patron, Isaac Taylor, waited upon me, and upon my telling him I was going to Newcastle, he enquired how long it would be before I returned. 'Never,' was my reply, at which he seemed both surprized and displeased. He then warmly remonstrated with me upon this impropriety of my conduct – told me of the prospects before me, and among many other matters, that of his having engaged me to draw in the Duke of Richmond's Gallery and [he] urged me strenuously to change my mind. I told him that no temptation of gain, of honour, or of any thing else, however great, could ever have any weight with me and that I would even enlist for a soldier – or go and herd sheep at five shillings per week as long as I lived, rather than be tied to live in London. I told him how sensible I was of his uncommon kindness to me and thanked him for it. My kind friend left me in the pet, and I never saw him more. He afterwards, when an old man, visited Newcastle, but left it again without my knowing it 'till after he was gone. At this I felt much grieved and disappointed. He did not live long after this – I do not remember how long – but a memoir of him was published in the *Literary Panorama* at the time, together with a letter I had written to him sometime before his death, which he never answered. He was in his day accounted the best engraver of embellishments for books, most of which he designed himself. The frontispiece to the first edition of Cunningham's* Poems, was one of his early productions, and at that time my friend Pollard and myself thought it the best thing that ever was done.

The same kind of persuasions were urged upon me by Mr Hodgson, to remain in London, as had been used by Mr Taylor – which ended in a similar way; he however went further and told me, if I was determined upon leaving London, and would continue to work for him in Newcastle, he would furnish me with plenty of it, and that he would begin by giving me as much as would keep me employed for two years. This was

* John Cunningham, the pastoral poet died September [18] 1773 Æ 43 years and was buried in St John's Church-yard Newcastle.

The Bean Goose NHSN

The Old Soldiers

The builder, less recently returned from the wars, still wears the tattered remnant of his uniform. See page 54 for Bewick's reference to Ben Garlick and John Cowie, the veterans of Minden. BM

A Ruined Church by the Sea

A scene probably inspired by the ruins of the old church at Alnmouth, later blown down by gales in 1806. BM

particularly pleasing to me because I could not bear the thoughts of beginning business in Newcastle in opposition to my old master, for whom I had the greatest respect – this to me appeared like 'bring up chickens to peck out your eyes'.

Having spent the evening 'till a late hour with my friends at 'The George' in Brook Street – and in the morning taken leave of my landlord and landlady (Mr and Mrs Kendal) and family, in Wharton's Court Holborn – I then posted off to the Pool and got on board of a collier, and after a very short passage, arrived in sight of St Nicholas Church steeple about the 22 June 1777.

8

The first thing after my arrival in Newcastle, was to see my old master, and the next to engage my old lodgings at Ned Hatfield's and to fit up a work bench in it, and then to set to work upon my wood cuts. This was however interrupted by other jobs, and the first of the kind was that of engraving a copper plate of the figure of the 'Theban Harp' for the Reverend James Murray* for some of his publications of which he was the author of several. Some of the silversmiths also began to press their jobs upon me. I had not, however, been long at work for myself, 'till proposals were made to me to join in partnership with my late master, and this was brought about by our mutual (friend?) John Robertson the silver-smith. This proposal, which was to set me down at once in a well established business, I did not relish so warmly as our mutual friend expected. I had formed a plan of working alone without any assistance from apprentices, or of being interrupted by any one, and I am not certain at this day whether I would not have been happier in doing so than in the way I was led to pursue. I had often, in my lonely walks, debated this business over in my mind, but whether it would have been for the better or the worse, I can now only conjecture – I tried the one plan and not the other. Perhaps each way might have had advantages and disadvantages. I would not have experienced the envy and ingratitude of some of my pupils, neither should I, on the contrary, have felt the pride and the pleasure I derived from so many of them having received medals or premiums from the Society for the Encouragement of Arts, and also of their taking the lead, as engravers on wood in the metropolis.

Notwithstanding this pride and this pleasure, I am inclined to think I should have had (ballancing the good against the bad) more pleasure in working alone for myself, than with such help as apprentices afforded, for with some of them I had a deal of turmoil and trouble; and others who shewed capacity and genious, and perhaps served out their time

---

* The Reverend James Murray, a Church of Scotland minister, with whom I had been long acquainted. He was accounted one of the best Hebrew scholars of his day, his 'Sermons to Asses' attracted much notice, and so did many of his other works. He was a keen satirical writer in some of his controversies. Among his friends he was of a lively, witty and pleasant temper, and greatly valued by a numerous acquaintance, who admired him for his humanity and good sense and much courted his company. He died in 28 January 1882 – aged 50 years – and was buried in St Andrew's Church yard.

without an interchange of a cross word between us, yet these, from coming under the guidance of people of an envious and malignant disposition perhaps in unison with their own, were, after every pains and every kindness had been shewn to them, when done, ready to strangle me. I have much reason to remember, on an occasion of my

partner and myself, being obliged to take one of the most impudent, malignant and worst apprentices we ever had, before the magistrates; one of them (John Erasmus Blackett Esqr) calling me to aside, to enquire if I knew his associates, I told him I did, and he sent for some of them, and in the mean time told me he never knew of any *bad* apprentices being brought before them, who had not been spoiled by the wicked advice of some worthless person or other. It is painful to me to dwell on a subject of this kind, which indeed I might spin out to a great length with much additional matter, but it may be sufficient to observe that I have taken a boy and behaved to him uniformly with the kindness of a father or a brother, and have watched with every pains in my power to instruct him – been liberal to him in pecuniary matters – employed the best physician to attend him when he was unwell – let him want for nothing – paid him his wages besides, whether at work or not at work, and in this my partner contributed his share – and along with myself used every endeavour in our power to advance him in the world, and when all this was done, he shewed not a particle of gratitude, but observed that any 'cartman would take care of his horse', and then put himself under the guidance and directions of a company or confedracy of ill disposed, envious and malignant persons, who after having laboured to poison the ears of the public and of the jury – to bring us to trial, for the pay for work done without the leave of his masters, while he was our apprentice! and the business was so managed that a verdict was given against us. I did not fail to attack this jury individually and to send the confiderates a message, that there was not a man among them who was not a coward and a scoundrel.

During my abscence in London, Mr Beilby had taken an apprentice, with a premium, and to make us equal, I took my brother John as mine. With my brother I was extremely happy – we lodged together, he arose early in the morning, lighted our fire, blacked our shoes, dusted the room, made every thing clean for breakfast, as well as any servant girl could have done, and he sewed and mended his own clothes etc and to crown all he was constantly cheerfull, lively and very active, and my friends were his friends. Mr Beilby was also as pleased with him as I could possibly be, for besides his affable temper, he took every kind of work in hand so pleasantly and so very soon learned to execute it well that it could not miss giving satisfaction, and this he continued to do as long as he was with us; but other parts of his conduct, when he arrived at manhood was not so well and gave me great uneasiness, for he got acquainted with company which I thought badly of, and my remonstrances to him respecting them proved in vain. He would not (as he called it) be dictated to by me, but this I persisted in 'till it made us often quarrel – this was distressing to me, for my regard for him was too deeply routed ever to think of suffering him to tread in the paths which led to ruin, without endeavouring to prevent it. To the latest day of his life he repented of his turning a deaf ear to my advise, and as bitterly and sincerely did he acknowledge the slightest obligations he owed me – he *rued*, and that is as painful a word as any in the English language.

As soon as I thought he might be able to work his way in the world, he having been (I think) about five years with me, I gave him his liberty, and he set off for London, where, from his reformed conduct, and where, from every information I could learn, he was much liked and respected. He was as industrious in London as he had been with us and had plenty of work to do – he was almost entirely employed by the publishers and booksellers in London, in designing and cutting an endless variety of blocks for them, and as he was extremely quick at his work, he did it slightly and at a very low rate for them. His too close confinement, however, impared his health and he revisited Cherryburn, where he did not remain long 'till he thought himself quite recovered and then he returned again to London where he continued a few years longer, and where the same kind of confinement, brought him down as before. A similar visit to his native air was found necessary, and where his health was again restored to him, and he again returned to London. He however found that he could not pursue the same kind of close confinement – on which account he engaged himself to teach the boys drawing at the Hornsey Academy, then kept by Mr Nathaniel Norton, which obliged him to keep a pony, on which he rode backwards and forward, and thus dividing his time between his work office in London and the school, for some few years. When his health began again to decline and he finally left London early in the summer of 1795, he returned once more to the banks of the Tyne, where he intended to follow the wood engraving for his London friends and particularly from William Bulmer, for whom he was engaged to execute a number of blocks for *Fabliaux or Tales* by Le Grand and for Somerville's *Chase*. Many of the former he (I believe) had finished (with assistants) in

London and had sketched others on the blocks which he finished at Cherryburn. He had also sketched the designs on the blocks for the *Chase* and these I put the finishing hand to after his decease – which happened on the 5 December 1795 – aged 35 years. The last thing I could do for him was putting up a stone to his memory in Ovingham Church yard – where I hope, when my *glass* is run out, to be laid down beside him.

While my brother was my apprentice, he frequently accompanied me on my weekly visits to Cherryburn. He was then a clever, springy youth, and our bounding along together was often compared to the scamperings of a pair of wild colts. These journeys commenced while I was an apprentice. I then went and returned on the same day, but when I became my own master, I seldom missed a week for years, and for many years throughout, 'in summer's heat and winter's freezing cold', I did not miss a single one week. When I was an apprentice I had a few days *holly days* at Easter and Whitsuntide allowed me, according to promise, and these were wholly employed in angling – but after the time came when I might do as I pleased, I mostly stopped when the weather suited in spring and summer, and spent the Mondays in various streams, at this my favourite and indeed only diversion. In this I was accompanied with my cheerfull assosiate Jack Roe, with his flies and his tackle, and when we had got a number sufficient, I returned that night or the next morning with my creel filled with fish, which I divided among friends in Newcastle. With an account of these hungry stream wading ramblings and the days spent in angling, and with a description of the beautiful scenery of water sides and the renovating charms which these together inspired, a volume might be filled, in imitation of the Patriarch of Anglers, Izaak Walton, as might also one of a descriptive or senti-mental journal of these my weekly visits to my parents. These visits continued regularly from 1777 till 1785, in which year my mother, my eldest sister and my father all died. It will readily be believed that if I had not felt uncommon pleasure in these journeys, I would not have persisted in them, nor in facing then the snow storms, the floods and the dark nights of so many winters. This to some appeared like insanity, but my stimulant, as well as my reward, was in seeing my father and my mother in their happy home, which I always reflected would have an end, and that the time would come when I would have no feelings of warm regard called up on their account. Besides these gratifications I felt others in observing the weekly changes of the long lengthened and varied year, which by being so measured out, appeared like liv-ing double one's time. *The Seasons* by the inimitable Thomson had charmed me much, but viewing them experimentally, much more so. To be placed in the midst of a wood in the night, in whirlwinds of snow, while the tempest howled above my head, was sublimity itself and drew forth aspirations to Omnipotence such as had not warmed my imagina-tion so highly before – but indeed, without being supported by extacies of this kind, the spirits, so beset, would have flagged and I should have sunk down. As soon as the days began to lengthen and the sprouting herbage had covered the ground, I often stopped with delight by the sides of woods, to admire the dangling woodbine and roses and the grasses, powdered, or spangled with pearly drops of dew – and also week after week, the continued succession of plants and wild flowers – the primrose, the wild hyacinths, the hare bell, the daisey, the cowslip, and these altogether I thought no painter ever could imitate. I had not at that time ever heard of the name of the great and good Linnaeus, and

knew only plants by their common English names. While admiring these beautifully enamelled spots on my way, I was also charmed with the equally beautifull little songsters which were constantly pouring out their various notes to proclaim the spring. While this exhilerating season glided on by imperceptable degrees, unfolding its blossoms 'till they faded into summer, and as the days lengthened, my hours of rising became more and more early. I have often thought that not one half of mankind knew any thing of the beauty, the serenity and the stillness of the summer mornings in the country, nor ever witnessed the rising sun's shining forth upon the new day. I had often listned with great pleasure and attention to my father's description of the morning, with his remarks upon the various wild quadrupeds and the strange birds he had seen or heard in these still hours throughout the year, for he left his bed very early in summer, and seldom later than 4 or 5 o'clock in the winter. The autumn I viewed as the most interesting season and in its appearance the most beautiful of the varied year – it is then that the yellow harvest of the fields and the produce of the orchards are gathered in as the rewards of the labours of the year – while the picturesque beauties and varying foliage of the fading woods with their falling leaves, and the assembling, in flocks, of the small birds, put me in mind of the gloomy months with which the year is closed.

This is the short account of many years of great and uninterrupted health, bouyant spirits and of great happiness to me. I had begun

[103]

betimes and by degrees, to habituate myself to temperance and exercise, which hardened the constitution to such a pitch that no wet, nor cold had any bad effect upon me. On setting out upon my weekly pedestrian *flights* up the Tyne, I never looked out to see whether it was a good day or a bad one – the worst that ever fell from the skies never deterred me from undertaking my journey. On setting out I always waded through the first pool I met with and had sometimes the river to wade at the far end. I never changed my cloaths, however they might be soaked with wet and though they might be stiffened by the frost on my returning home at night, 'till I went to bed. I had inured myself to this hardihood, by always sleeping with my windows open, where a thorough air, as well as the snow blew through my room – in this I lay down, stripped into *bare buff* except being rolled in a blanket, upon a mattrass as hard as I could make it. Notwithstanding this mode of treating myself, I never had any ailment, even in the shape of a cold, while I continued to live in this way, nor did I experience any difference, untill, when married, I was obliged to alter my plan and to live and behave like other folks. To persons brought up in and habituated to the tender indulgencies common in the world, the mode of life I have been describing, would (perhaps) not be believed; and if any such, who were not brought up to bear it by degrees in the same way, were unprepared to try the experiment – it *would be at their peril*. My travelling expences for the day was commonly only a penny or two pence for crossing the water. On the hottest day I was never made violently to perspire and commonly only felt a dampness on my brow. I carried no useless weight of fat about me and the muscular parts were as hard as it was possible to be on any human being. On being asked by a gentleman, an acquaintance, who I met with in Ovingham, what I got to drink on such hot days on my road, my reply was – nothing; he had not been used to such doings himself, and was surprized, and could hardly believe me. He then earnestly persuaded me to try the experiment of the amazing good a glass of brandy and water wou'd do me in hot weather; this I took no notice of for some time – at length, however, on a thundery hot day, on my being scorched with heat, and threatned with being struck with the lightning which darted from a sky almost as black as ink, I stepped into a public house in Crawcrook, and for the first time in my life, called for a glass of brandy and water. I was then about 28 years old – and surely I thought this brandy and water was the most delicious beverage in the world. This would not be worth noticing, but only on account of its being a beginning to me, and which I did not, when occasion pressed me, leave off for some years afterwards. I often called in, almost every Sunday morning, for my glass, while my rout lay on that side of the river, and untill being *quized* for visiting 'Maggy Hay's bonney lasses'. I then left off and walked up the north side of the Tyne and crossed at Wylam, Ovingham or Eltringham Boat, and now only sometimes at Scotchwood when I had occasion to visit my friends at Hedley – but indeed I varied my roundabout ways in these journeys, pursuing the one I had haunted myself to, for perhaps a quarter of a year to an end, before I left it off, and thus became known to most of the villages on both banks of the Tyne; and as nothing can pass unnoticed in villages – so they noticed me and set it down for granted that I was sweethearting some pretty female on my way. This life of raptureous enjoyment has its acids and at length comes to an end, and so did my walks and my reflections or contemplations which passed through the mind while engaged in them – these at the time were mostly communicated to a moralizing and sensibly religious friend, Joseph Hubbuck, who waited my return on the Sunday evenings, when over our supper of a pint of ale and a cake, for each – he in return detailed to me the import of the sermons he had heard through the day.

9

In Christmas week 1784, while I was on some errand to Ovingham, amusing myself with sliding on the ice, as smooth almost as a seeing glass, between Eltringham and that place – I know not what came over my mind, but something ominous haunted it, of a gloomy change in the family taking place. At this I was surprized, for I had never before felt any such sensation and presently scouted it as some whim of the imagination. It was to be a day of cheerfulness, for Mr and Mrs Storey distant relations of my father, and for whom my parents had the greatest regard, had been, with other friends invited to dine with us at Cherryburn that day. At dinner all was kindness and cheerfulness and my father was as usual, full of his jokes and telling some of his fecetious stories and anecdotes. For two or perhaps three Sundays after this, I was prevented from getting over the water by the ice and other floods, and returned from Ovingham without seeing or hearing how all were at home. The Sunday after upon making my constant call at John Gilchrist's, the gardner in Ovingham – where, when at school, we always left our dinner poke and dined – he informed me with looks of grief, that my mother was very unwell. I posted off in haste, along with him, and across the river to see her. Upon my asking her earnestly how she was, she took me apart by myself, and told me it was nearly all over with her and described to me how she had 'got her death' – she had been called up in a severe frosty night, to see a young woman in the hamlet below, who was taken ill, and thinking the bog she had to pass through at the nearest, might be frozen hard enough to bear her, she slumped deep into it and before she waded through it she got very wet and a perishment of cold, and in that state she went to give her advice about what was best to be done with her patient. I employed my friend Dr Bailes to visit her and I ran up from Newcastle two or three times a week with his medicines for her – but all would not do. She died on the 20 February 1785 aged 58 years. She was possessed of great innate powers of mind, which had been cultivated by her own endeavours as well as by a good education; for these and for her benevolent humane disposition and good sense she was greatly respected and, indeed, revered by the whole neighbourhood. My eldest sister, Hannah Chambers, who was down from London on a visit to her home, at the time of my mother's illness and death, had by her over exertions and anxiety, brought on a miscarriage and became very ill, and for the convenience of medical aid and better nursing, I brought her to my hitherto happy little cot at the Forth, where she died on the 24th of June 1785 aged 30 years. These were gloomy days to me. Some short time before my sister died, upon her requesting me and my promising her that I would see her buried at Ovingham, she proposed to sing me a song – I thought this very singular, and at it felt both sorrow and surprize – but she smiled at me and began her song of 'all things have but a time'. I had heard the old song before, and thought pretty well of it, but hers was a later and a very much better version of it. During this time I observed a great change in the looks and deportment of my father, he had what is called 'never held up his head' since the death of my mother, and upon my anxiously pressing him to tell me what ailed him, he said he had felt, as if he were shot through from the breast to the shoulders, with a great pain that hindered him from breathing freely, and upon my mentioning medical assistance, he rejected it and told me if I sent him any druggs, I might depend up[on] it he would throw them all behind the fire. He wanderd about all summer alone, with a kind of serious look and took no pleasure in any thing, 'till near the 15 of November, which I understand was his birth day and on which he completed his 70th year, and on that day he died and was buried beside my mother and sister at Ovingham. After this I left off my walks to Cherrybourn – the main attractions to it were gone and it became a place, the thoughts of which now raked up sorrowfull reflections in my mind. Having left out some particulars respecting my father and illustrative to some peculiarities of his character, which may perhaps not be thought uninteresting, I shall give a few of such as I recollect. In his person he was a stout square made, strong and active man, and through life was a pattern of health. I was told by some of my aunts, who were older than him, that he never was ill from a disease in his life. I have heard him say '*he wondered how folks were, when they we[re] bad*'. He was of a very cheerful temper, and possessed an uncommon vein of humour and a fund of anecdote – and was by the gentlemen and others of the neighbourhood, much noticed for these as well as for his integrity. He had however, some traits that might be deemed singular and not in order – he never would prosecute any one for thefts, he hated going to law, but he took it at his own hand, and now and then gave thieves a severe beating and sometimes otherwise punishd them in a singular and whimsical way. I have known him, on a winter's night, rise suddenly up from his seat, and with a stick in his hand, set off to the coal pit in order to catch the depredators who he might detect, stealing his coals. I remember one instance of his thus catching a young fellow, a

[107]

farmer, with his loaded fother and of his giving him a severe beating, or
what was called a 'hideing' and of making him leave his booty, and go
home empty. The thieves themselves were sure to keep the business
secret and he himself never spoke of it bejond his own fire side. In these
robberies, which he saw with his own eyes, he conceived he did not need
the help of either witnesses, judge or jury, nor the occasion to employ
any attorney to empty his pockets. I have sometimes heard him make
remarks upon people, who he knew to be hypocrites, and on their loud
praying and holding up their hands in the church. After noticing one of
these at church one Sunday acting in this way, and of his remaining to
take the sacrament, some person called in on the afternoon with the
news of this very man's having, on his way home, caught poor Tommy
Cook the shoemaker's Galloway, which had gone in through a gap in
the hedge, into one of his fields, and that he had driven it before him
into the pinfold. This was sufficient – this was the spark, which kindled
up and increased to a blaze, which my father could not muster temper
enough [to] keep down – and next morning he set off to the smith's shop
and sent for this choleric, purse proud man, to whom in rude terms he
opened out upon, about his finished hypocracy – and at length insisted
upon and obliged him immediately to release the Galloway from its
hungry imprisonment, and further that he should instantly go and make
his peace with this poor but honest and much respected man; he further
strongly recommended to him to go no more to church to shout and
pray, nor to take the sacrament 'till a change of conduct took place in his
mind – and that he ought, that very night, before he slept, to sit down
on his bare knees, and implore forgivness of the God of truth, justice and mercy for his past crimes. The last transaction on this subject I
shall mention and which bore a more serious complexion than the

[108]

foregoing, happened while I was an apprentice – a pitman of the name of George Parkin, who had long wrought in the colliery and was highly valued by my father for his industry sobriety and honesty – he would not do any thing unfairly in working the coal in the boards himself, nor suffer others to do so. For this conduct he became deservedly a great favourite – so much so that one of the old lodges had been comfortably fitted up for him and his family to live in, without rent, and a garth besides was taken in off the common for his use. With these he often expressed himself so highly pleased, that he used to say he was happier than a prince. My father for many years – ever, indeed, since the gin once ran amain, and in his attempting to stop it, he got his scull fractured – had made it a point, if possible, to let the men down to their work himself, so that he saw that all was safe with his own eyes. All passed on pleasantly in this way for a long while, 'till one morning when he was thus to be employed. In letting down the men, George was always the first man to his work, and having fixed himself in the chain, with his son on his arm to be both let down together, he had given the signal 'wiseaway'; at the same time holding up his 'low rope' he observed the pit rope which was to bear their weight had been cut near the chain – on this he shouted 'stop!' and started back upon the '*seddle boards*' just in time to prevent their being precipitated to the bottom of the pit. He was like to be over powered with the shock when my father, keeping the dreg upon the 'Start' caught hold of him and the boy and conducted them both into the lodge; he then examined the rope and found it had been cut through to the last strand and he then stopt the working of the pit for that day. Poor Geordy, in great distress of mind, set off to Newcastle to inform me of what had happened. I was grieved to hear his tale and this was heightened by his declaring that all his pleasures were at an end, for he could never go back to his work, nor to his happy home again. For sometime my father seemed lost in pondering over this misterious affair in his mind; he however at length began to be fixed in his suspicions and as was usual on such occasions, his indignation step by step rose to the greatest height. In this state of mind he set off unusually soon to let the men down to their work, knowing that the subject of his suspicion, a wicked, ignorant young fellow, would that morning be the first and alone – he began by accusing him of the horrid deed and then instantly to give him a severe beating and overpowered him, and then made him believe he would drag him to the pit and throw him down the shaft if he did not confess. The threat succeeded – he was affraid for his life, and he confessed, and my father then instantly dismissed him from his employment. When the rest of the men came, they saw, by the blood and the retaliating blows on his face that something had been the matter – he then told them the particulars, at which they felt eased in their own minds and greatly rejoiced. In this state of things, the accusing *culprit*, while he bore the marks of violence upon him, set crippling off to lodge his complaint to the justices – and my father was summonzed to appear before them. When met together the justices, Captains Smith and Bainbridge,* of the Riding, heard the charge for the assault, which from the first appearance of the complainant before them they had no reason to doubt about it. They then both expressed their surprize, to find my father, with whom they had been in habits [of] neighbourly intimacy, and who was the last man on earth they could suspect as capable of committing such an outrage, and after laying down the law in such cases, they wished to hear what he had to say for himself. He readily acknowledged what he had done and his reasons for doing so – they then seemed much shocked at the horrid narrative, and after confering together in private a short time, the business was resumed – and 'Pray,' said one of them – 'Were not you the very man, who robbed Bywell Lock?' and then, looking him sternly in the face – 'and was not this master of yours the very friend, by whose unceasing endeavours and influence you were saved from transportation? – Begon! leave the country and let us never see you more.' He left the country for many years, and on his return I was both pleased and surprized to find he was a very reformed man. (In addition to this long account, I must add that my father could not be troubled to harbour ill will in his mind and that if he was passionate he was equally compassionate.)

* Now Major Bainbridge – who has been many years in the commission of the peace, in which he has been much respected both as a magistrate and a man. Without knowing any thing about what side he took in politics, I have always considered him as a local patriot – keen in promoting every thing for the benefit of Tyne side. While I am writing this (23 June 1823) he is now living and in his 87th year. Captain Smith I did not know. Major Bainbridge died 6 December 1826 in his 91st year.

10

For many years past, including a part of those of my apprenticeship, we were fully employed upon such work as I have named before, from silversmiths, hardwaremen and watchmakers – but a new customer (Isaac Hymen, a Jew) came early into notice, with his seal cutting orders, which amounted to more in that way than all the rest put together. This man besides his box of watches, trinkits etc, had got gathered together a great collection of impressions of well cut seals, and being a man of good address and a good singer, he introduced himself into coffee rooms frequented by gentlemen and respectable tradesmen, and there he exhibitted his impressions as the work of his own hands, and by his own good management (for he knew nothing whatever of engraving of any kind) he got his orders – and somehow or other it was well propagated through the town that his seals surpassed by far, any thing we ever did or could do, and though we had done the whole of his orders, yet this was believed and there seemed [to be] only one opinion as to his very superior excellence. I remember of once rising early in the morning and working 'till late at night, and in that day of cutting five steel seals, with cyphers, or initials – for which our common charge, wholesale was 3/6 and to our own customers, five shillings. For these he charged 12s or 12s/6d each to his friends. He observed to me, upon my telling him of his extravagant charges, that it was 'foolish in us to do as we did' – but for himself he said 'you know I must live'. My wages for the short time I worked for my late master after I was out of my apprenticeship, was a guinea per week – but Isaac offered me two, if I would travel with him. The travelling part, I liked well enough, but not that of travelling with a Jew. He went on in this way with his orders, till we had no other customer and my master, then as well as when I became his partner, often expressed himself highly chagrined, that even some of his old private friends went past him and even joined others in lessening our work. Our *friend Isaac* continued long uninterruptedly thus *to carry all before him*, 'till some of our old customers became irritated at him, and particularly John Harrison, the watch maker, who seemed to do nothing besides that of going about to open out and expose the business. Isaac then left Newcastle and common report said he was found dead on the road between Sunderland and Durham. I have often seen in London, and perhaps the same may be seen in every large town, 'the pale artist ply his sickly trade' to keep in affluence such managing, money making, pretended artists, something like Isaac Hymen – and this must continue to be the case so long as gentlemen will not be at the pains to encourage merit and to go themselves to the *fountain head* for their nice jobs. Our main supporters in the silver engraving were John Langlands and his partner John Robertson. Before they entered into partnership Mr Robertson was well known and much respected in almost every principal town in Britain and (I believe) in Ireland, as a travelling silversmith and jeweller and by his superiour knowledge of business he greatly augmented that of their joint concern. Mr Langlands was of a cheerfull, hospitable and charitable disposition, and full of stories and anecdotes, and that kind of man who greatly esteemed men of ability, integrity and industry – these he never forgot when age or infirmities brought them down – he then shook hands with them as he had done before, but now his own mostly concealed his token of respect – a half guinea. Mr Robertson was also, in many respects, of a similar disposition as his partner. I spent many a cheerfull evening in Mr Langlands' house with these kind friends, in company with others who also partook of his hospitable board, but the most remarkable of these was Matthew Prior, who had the character of being one of the best mechanics in the kingdom. He was Assay Master, musical instrument maker and a turner, in which last he particularly excelled: many remarkable pieces of dextrous workmanship he had done in that way, which drew him into the notice of many gentlemen in the two northern counties, with whom also as an angler, a sportsman and a jovial companion he was their welcome guest. It happened on some pretence or other, that an attempt was made to take away the Assay business from Newcastle, which occasioned Prior's being sent for to be examined by (I believe) a committee of the House of Commons, as to his ability etc of conducting that business. The ease, the clearness, as well as the streight forward way in which he answered all questions, excited some surprize as well as approbation. He at last, when he was questioned as to the accuracy of his scale beam, told them that a hair clipped from the back of his hand, would cast his scales either way, and this was actually true. For a wager he turned two billiard balls of such equal weights that the difference was as nothing. He was of a most independent cast of character and open and frank in his conversation – upon one occasion it had been reported that Prior, should have said of a proud high minded gentleman, that he 'durst do what neither the gentleman nor any of his family durst do'. Prior had never said any such thing, but this gentleman took him to task about it with great indignation and accused him of saying so; at this Prior in his turn felt offended and told him 'tho he had never said so, he

Boys and Toy Ships

*A scene perhaps reminiscent of Bewick's childhood, when he built dams
and sailed toy boats in the Colliers' Close burn above Cherryburn.* BM

The Dog and Saucepan

*The scene depicts a cruel sport not uncommon in Bewick's time amongst
idle boys in country places. The principal figure was modelled on a
tanner known to Bewick who worked near the Westgate, Newcastle.* IB

The Runaway Cart

*The attractions of the ale house had proved too powerful for the driver,
to the delight of the idle boys.* B M

A Roadman Breaking Stones B M

would say so to his face now. This produced a wager between them and Matthew told him he would double the bet if he pleased. 'Now,' said the gentleman in high ill humour, 'and what is it you dare do!' – 'Do' said Prior – 'I dare spend the last sixpence I have in the world.'

During [a] great part of the time and the transactions I have been noticing, the American War was going on. The Press broke out just after I landed in London, and to escape the gang, one of our crew came and took refuge with me. This poor fellow, a decent man, had in his

youth been on board of a ship of war and as far as concerned himself he said he did not mind going again, but the thoughts of being digged from his family threw him into very great distress. Political writings and debatings sometimes ran very high between those who were advocates for a system of corruption and profited by the taxes – and those who were advocates for the liberties of mankind – but it always appeared to me that a very great majority of the people were decidedly against the war. These writings and debatings which the war occasioned, certainly served greatly to alter the notions and the opinions of the people respecting the purity of the British government and its representative system, and this attempt at doing it away altogether in America seemed a prelude or forerunner to the same system of misrule, when by slower degrees, a future opportunity offered of doing it away at home. In this state of political debatings, the question was often asked 'whether the Government was made for the people or the people for the Government?' and this seemed very feebly to be answered – but great numbers, who hoped for the best, still clung to the Government under which they had been brought up and had been taught to revere as excellency itself. While others were contending whether a kingly Government or a Republic were best, it was admitted that a deal might be said pro and con, for many examples might be produced of maladministration under both forms; then some of these disputants would repeat what Pope had said, 'for modes of faith let graceless Zelots fight – 'his can't be wrong whose life is right – 'For forms of Government, it is confessed – 'That which is best administered, is best.' In England the people may boast that their forefathers had a King, in 'Alfred the Great' the wisest the bravest and the best, the world ever knew, and by whose whole excellent conduct was laid the foundation of the liberties of his country from the influence of which, there can be no doubt that the English language will be spoken over almost the whole globe. Were kings to endeavour to follow his example and ever keep in mind, that they and their ministers ought to consider themselves as a Royal society for the promotion of arts and sciences and of every thing that can enlighten the minds and ameliorate the condition of their subjects, they would then do right. Were this the case, Kings would reign in the hearts of the great over whelming mass of the people, which no confedracy or conspiracy of nobles or others could ever upset; but while they continue to suffer themselves to be surrounded by flatterers, sycophants and selfish knaves, no good nead be expected, for they are thus brought up like petted children and have not the same chance left them of becoming wise like other men. Thus situated they are to be pittied. One would think that the respectable part of the old nobility, or other opulent men of great abilities might be found with patriotism enough to do the offices of the ministry gratis, scouting high saleries and only looking to honourable distinction – this would of itself put an end to corruption. Justices of the peace take the very great trouble of acting their parts gratuitously, church wardens and overseers do the same, and why [do] not the great and rich men of the land follow the praiseworthy example.

In reverting back to take another look at this war, one may reckon to a certainty of its having been made the subject of debatings and of furnishing matter for the thinking part of mankind, over the whole of the civilized world. George the third and his advisers did not perhaps think of this nor its consequences, neither did they ever contemplate upon the mighty events they were bringing about in thus rearing and establishing the wisest and greatest republic and nation the world ever saw – which, when its immense territory is filled with an enlightened population and its government like a rock founded on the liberties and the rights of man, it is bejond human comprehension to foresee the strides they will make towards perfection; and it is likely they will cast a compassionate eye on the rest of the world grovelling under arbitrary power, banish it from the face of the earth, and kill despots with a frown.*

* Thus far, from page 35 [p. 51 of this book] was written, while confined by a fit of the gout, at home, from 29 May till 24 June 1823.

To prevent this, one would fain hope that kings and their advisers would coolly reflect upon the improving intellect of mankind, and take measures to govern them accordingly and in a way more befitting the state of the people over whom they are called upon to rule.

During the long continuance of this war and the debatings, as before noticed, I got acquainted with a number of genteel young men† of a literary turn, who kept a library of books and held their meetings in a room at Sam Alcock's, at the Sign of the Cannon, at the foot of the old Flesh Market – and I used to frequent this house in the evenings, to get

my pint of ale and a cake and to hear the news, and to have a bit of chat or conversation with some of them when they adjourned from their book society. I did not join them in this society, but I sometimes dined with them at their annual cheerfull dinner. I was never fond of dinners or dining parties, and I think I would not have partaken with them had I not been tempted to do so, by way of hearing their songs, with which I felt much charmed, but particularly with the Scotch songs with which one of their members, Walter Cannaway, the carver and gilder, used so highly to delight the company; on these occasions he, according to my notions of singing, was the best I ever heard. I had always been more charmed with the human voice, when well attuned, than with any instrumental music whatever, and Cannaway's voice was extremely good. He could in a natural tone go to the highest and the lowest pitch, with his pauses, his shakes or quavers – all in time. Many others, perhaps, who might have as good a voice and as correct an ear for music as him, would have been equally as charming, had they not been spoiled by the fashion they had got into, to please the surfeited tastes of

† Joseph Hubbuck, woollen draper, Moses Marshall, cashier and at the Bank, John Gale, Sword Bearer, Gilfrid Ward (of facetious memory) woollen draper and many others of an intelligent, chearfull and pleasant character.

coxcomical connoiseurs and a vitiated aping public. I have ever been much disgusted to hear and see one of these spoiled performers, quavering and spinning out his or her assumed unnatural falsetto voice untill he or she was almost spent. It shewed well how long winded these kind of performers were, but I never could sit to hear any of them – as it appeared to me to be any thing but music – or music run mad.

On my first coming to business, I had an opportunity of sometimes hearing musical concerts. My master belonged to a musical society held at Moore's in the Close and when I had any message to take, or other errand to him, I was commonly invited to remain. The two sons (Edward and Charles) of Charles Avison, the great musical composer, belonged to this society and Mr Beilby and family were on terms of intimacy with them. I also occasionly heard the band at the Theatre, but I cannot say I felt much pleasure in listning to them, and I well remember, on one occasion, of setting them aside: the late Mr Dibden, who often called upon me, had some performance to exhibit at our Theatre, and had quarrelled with the theatrical band, on account of their exorbitant demands and in this delemma he expressed himself to me how much he felt disappointed and knew not what to do. I told him, I thought if he would leave the matter to me, I could set all right, and instantly applied to old William Lamshaw, the Duke of Northumberland's Piper, to ask him if he thought he could engage to play at the Theatre that night; being well acquainted with the old man he readily assented. I then told my friend Dibden of what I had done, and satisfied him, as to the preference the audience would give to the piper – in this I was not mistaken, for all went well off and every one expressed both pleasure and surprize at the change.

For sometime before the American War broke out, there had been a lack of musical performers in our streets and in this kind of interval, I used to contrive to get into the company, or to engage John Peacock, our inimitable performer, to play on the Northumberland or small pipes, and with his old tunes, his lilts, his pauses and his variations, I was always excessively pleased. At one time I was affraid that these old tunes and this ancient instrument, might from neglect of encouragement get out of use, and I did every thing in my power to prevent this, and to revive it again by urging Peacock to teach pupils to become masters of this kind of music – and I am vain enough to believe that my efforts were not lost. I was suspicious that the Northumberland family were beginning to feel indifferent or to overlook and slight these their ancient minstrels, who had for ages past been much esteemed by their forefathers and kept in attendance upon them.

It was however, with great pleasure I found that they had appointed William Cant, (a pupil of old William Lamshaw) to be piper to the Northumberland Regiment of Militia and he kept up with great spirit and effect this department of their music, while he remained in the regiment.* And it seems that the other departments of their music were not behind Cant in this respect, for it was allowed by judges that their fifers and drummers were inferiour to none in the kingdom – one man in particular, John Bowman, it was asserted, was the best performer on the fife that was 'known in the world'. Certain it is, however, that he chalenged the fifers of every regiment who were stationed in Newcastle, to a trial of skill on that instrument, every year for twenty two years – but none of them could compete with him. He could draw out tones from it the most soft and graceful, as well as the most stunning and loud, such as the ear could not endure in a room, and which was only fit to be heard in the open air.

* July 15 1821 – Died Mr William Cant, master of Blue Bell, head of the Side, Newcastle, aged 70 years, formerly piper to the Northumberland Militia. He was an excellent performer on the violin and the Northumberland pipes; and like his great predecessors on the latter instrument, Turnbull, Gilley, old Lamshaw and Peacock, he kept up the ancient tunes, with all their charming lilts and pauses, unspoiled by the *modern improvers* of music, with their 'Idiot Notes impertinently long'. He played 'his native Wood Notes wild', such as pleased the ears of the yeomanry of old, at Otterburn, Hedgley Moor, and Flodden field. For

> *Whene'er his pipe did silence break*
> *You'd thought the Instrument would speak*

When Cant died, I sent the above to Mr Walker's paper, but am not certain whether I sent the distich at the end or not. T. Bewick.

11

I have hitherto noticed several of my friends and acquaintances whose characters stood high in my estimation. I have now another to introduce, the play fellow of my youth, Thomas Lawson, as remarkable as any of them. He left Tyne side, his and my home and came to Newcastle about the year 1777 or 1778 to launch out into the world of exertion and turmoil, and from his abilities and great integrity he seemed well befitted to make a great figure in it, and had he been spared, he would in my opinion have shone out like another Benjamin Franklin. He was for a short time one of my schoolfellows at Ovingham. From his father's having been beggar'd by the faileur of a great coal owner, for whom he had been employed for many years, his mother brought up a large family with the small profits of a public house, the Sign of the White Horse, in Ovingham. The house was his father's, but the brewer got it for what was owing to him for ale. This brewer however, being a generous man, still did not take the house as his own, but permitted the family to keep it for the support of themselves and some of the younger children. My young friend was obliged to leave school and to seek out some employment for himself. In the interem he took up his abode in my father's house as a home – his mother having been much respected by my mother and between whom a close intimacy had long subsisted. The first employment that my companion got, was that of a plough driver – then a farmer's servant – then a manager of a farm, and the last he held in the country, was of a two fold nature in which he had to look after the concern of a farm and a brewery. In all these departments, he was greatly distinguished, for his industry, his good sense, good management and great integrity. It however happened, he being handsome in his person and manly in his looks and deportment, his employer began to suspect that the young lady of the house was shewing a marked partiality towards him, and this having occasioned some frowns and some hints, which his spirit could not brook, he gave up the place. Having seen an advertisement from a gentleman going on his travels, who wanted a young man as a servant and a manager of his affairs, poor Lawson was struck with this as a thing worth looking after and he immediately set off to Newcastle, to make the proper enquiries, and for that purpose, waited upon Mr Slack, bookseller and editor of the Newcastle Chronicle. As soon as he entered the shop or office Mrs Slack eyed him from head to foot, and after a short pause, she broke silence and began by telling him she thought it a great pity that such a young man, as he appeared to be, should not do better than putting himself to be a gentleman's servant, and asked him if would not like better to be [put to] some trade or business* – this he readily admitted, but at the same time observed that he had not the means of doing so. To this, being a very sensible, cleaver woman, she told him she would endeavour to help him to accomplish this, and after some bargain making, it was agreed, that he was, for a few years to be bound to Mr Slack as a pressman, for which he was to be paid eight shillings per week. At that time, and with this wage, he contrived to maintain himself, and also to pay out of it for a night school education, under the Reverend John Bailie,† and his progress in this way was truely astonishing, both in the languages and in figures, the use of the globes etc. But his memory was such that he retained what ever he learned, and could repeat the longest harangue (as far as I am able to judge) verbatim from end to end. I once had an opportunity of witnessing this, in his repeating the whole of a charity sermon, preached by the eloquent, the Reverend Dr Scott of Simonburn. While he was employed in the drudgery of the printing press, he at the same time made himself master of the business of compositor, and presently became a secondary foreman or manager under Robert Carr‡ who had long conducted the business in that office. I do not recollect how long Lawson remained in Mr Slack's employment, but shortly after he left him, he married a young woman of respectable parents, who had long been in love with him. It happened that the printing of a Bible in numbers had been established, but the editor, either from his mismanagement or something amiss, was on the verge of a faileur. In this state of things, Lawson turned his attention to this business, and applied to his wife's friends for assistance, but they could at that time only spare him about thirty pounds; with this sum in hand, he made his proposals for purchasing the types and every thing belonging to the printing office. It is singular enough that at this time, this printer (having left Newcastle) lived in and had his printing office in the Governor's House at Tynemouth, and I went down with my friend to this house, when the bargain was closed

* She selected and published *The Pleasing Instructor* – was the author of *Fisher's Grammar etc* and was quite a literary character.
† Reverend John Bailie, author of [*Lectures on the Revelations, Impartial History of Newcastle*, 1801, etc.] died [in Gateshead 12 December 1806] aged [66].
‡ Mr Carr was a man of great literary attainments and was considered as respectable for his talents as a poet – he was the friend and associate of Cunningham. [He died 4 June 1783, aged 45.]

[119]

between them. He now commenced printer on his own account, but how long he had to strugle through great difficulties before he got the business well established, I have forgot; but it is remarkable that he met with unsolicited aid from many friends, for every one who knew him became interested in his welfare. He lived untill he surmounted every obstacle to his prosperity, but in doing this, his too great application and exertions ruined his health. He pined away and died (in a house close by mine at the Forth) on the 7th of March 1783 aged thirty one years. I, with many other of his friends accompanied his remains to Ovingham, where he was buried. This was the first time in my life that I felt poignant grief.

My old schoolfellow and friend, Philip Gregson of the Custom House, London, being on a visit to his relatives and friends in the north in 1780, and I being always fond of rambling, proposed setting him on his return home, as far as York, if he would walk with me to that city, to which he agreed. We set off, and after spending a day or two with him there, we parted. I then took the road by Borough-Bridge to Ripon, where I stayed a short time 'till I had viewed the country around it and particularly Studley Park and its beautiful scenery. I then returned to Darlington, and changed my rout to the westward by Barnard Castle, Bowes, over Stainmore to Brough, Appleby and Penrith – and from thence to my uncle's at Ainstable. On leaving him and his family, I walked home that day to Cherrybourn and so on the next to Newcastle. As I have not interlarded this journey with any of my remarks on the road – the grandeur of York Minster – the large upright stones (called I believe the Devil's Arrows) near Boroughbridge – the extensive prospects from Cross Fell etc, and therefore my dear Jane must regard the whole of this merely as one of my *Tramps*, and a description of these places by others, may be referred to.

In another of my projected perambulations, I prevailed on my acquaintance Walter Cannaway to accompany me. We set off on an

[120]

Easter Sunday morning in 1784, by the sea side to Berwick and did not halt untill we arrived at Chevington, bejond Widdrington. I had not broke my fast and was quite ready to make a hearty meal upon some dry barley cake and cheese, while my thirsty companion was with equal pleasure enjoying himself with hearty draughts of ale. We reached Lesbury in the afternoon, and when my fellow traveller sat down, he observed that I might go on if I pleased but that he would not move a foot further that night. Next day, after sauntering a little about in the villages on our road, we reached Elwick, the hospitable mansion of my friend Thomas Younghusband Esqr, where we stopped that night. Mr Younghusband happening to have a few of his friends to spend the evening with him, they got on to make all merry and to singing songs, and when it came to Cannaway's turn, they begged he wou'd favour them in this way – he readily did so with his usual ease and ability. At his performance they were both so agreably surprized and pleased, that the company from his so entertaining them did not seperate 'till the morning. And that day we set off for Berwick, where after getting some refreshment and viewing the town etc, we returned again to Elwick by Holy Island. In the performance of this day's journey we had to encounter some difficulties which might have been attended with fatal consequences. We had been cautioned, after a certain hour, against attempting to undertake walking across the extensive flat, left bare by the ebb tide, and in doing this we were bejond the time named, and had to run the greatest part of the way and it was well we did so, for before we reached the island we found the tide was rapidly advancing between us and the shore, and we had to wade deeply before we reached it. On looking back, over the flat space we had just left, we were surprized to view it as a sea. My companion, being rather corpulent was in a sad state of perspiration with over exertion, and I think I was not much better from the anxiety I felt for him, while I was constantly urging him to mend his speed. We now hastened, dripping with wet, to a public house, where he eagerly took a few glasses of gin and prevailed upon me to take one, along with him, and this was the first glass of that liquor I recollect of ever having taken before. Our next business was to get a boat to set us across the arm of the sea between the island and the nearest shore towards Elwick; it was then nearly dark, and before the boatmen got us rowed across it was quite so. Where they landed us we knew not, but we had to wade to the dry beach. In shaping our course to Elwick we lost ourselves in the fields, and it was late before we arrived there. We were in as dirty a state as wet and mire could make us – Mrs Younghusband however lost no time in fitting us up with dry clothes and making us as comfortable as she could. After remaining a day or two at Elwick and making some visits along with Mr Younghusband in the neighbourhood, my fellow traveller had somewhat similar visits to pay, in collecting some debts due to him, which when done he met me at Alnwick – where Mr Younghusband, having to attend a meeting of the freeholders on some election business at the Town Hall, I accompanied him thither. Never having heard any speaches made before, I was much entertained in hearing those now made upon this occasion. This being about the time that Mr Pitt came into the administration, and being the son of the great Chatham, most people hoped and expected he would follow the bright, the patriotic example that had been set him – but one gentleman appearing to differ in opinion from the majority of the audience, and in what I conceived, an eloquent speech, foretold that he would turn out in character to be a quite different kind of man.

Sometime about the year [1790] I used occasionly to attend the social meetings held in the evening and which for many years afterwards was held at the 'Black Boy' and then called Swarley's Club, and in a short time I became a more regular member of it. This was the most rational society or meeting I ever knew – the few rules which bound us together were only verbal, and the first one was this, that it was expected every member should behave with decorum and like a gentleman – if any one transgressed in this point, he was immediately fined – if he did not comply with this, he was 'sent to Coventry', or perhaps dismissed; on entering the room, every Member paid down fourpence, which was to be spent in beer only, and any Member might introduce his friend, at the same expense. There was no fines for non attendance and no regular debatings allowed on any subject – nor any other debatings but such as might occasionally arise out of the passing conversation; and the club was ended at ten o'clock. George Carlton, was perpetual President, and in that office always conducted himself in a pleasant and gentlemanly manner; William Preston, the printer, was secretary and treasurer and always acquitted himself in the same agreable way as the President had done. Conversations among the friends, thus associated, consisting of merchants or respectable tradesmen, was carried on without restraint – and only interrupted for the moment while the President claimed their attention to listen to any particular news of the day that might be worth notice. Such a place of meeting proved greatly convenient and pleasant to many a stranger, who visited the town, and the expense was as nothing to them. It may seem strange, that out of a fourpenny club like this, there was commonly an overplus left, to give away at Xmas and Easter, to some charitable purpose. I went to this

Club, when I had time to spare, in an evening, and seldom missed a week to an end. This happy society was however at length broken up, at the time when the war on behalf [of] despotism was raging and the spy system was set afloat – some spies, and others of the same stamp contrived to get themselves introduced and to broach political questions for the purpose of exciting debates and feeling the pulse of the company, which before this had very seldom touched upon debates of this kind.

Besides being kept busy with the routine of the business of our work office, I was often engaged in executing wood cuts for publishers and printers, the dates of which at this moment, I do not recollect, but they were done at various times from about the year 1788 – to 1790 – but the first, of any importance, was the wood cuts of Roman Alters etc and the Arms of the Bishops of Durham, for Hutchinson's *History of Durham*, in which my friend the late George Allen Esqr of the Grange, Darlington took a conspicuous part. A set of cuts were done for Goldsmith's *Deserted Village*, for Mr Walker, printer of Hereford. Mr Nicholson, printer of Ludlow and Poughnill, the publisher of elegant selections from various authors, employed me to embellish some of these with wood cuts, but I at this time have quite forgot what I did for him. My old friend Mr Bulmer, of the Shakspere Printing Office, London, also employed me to execute the cuts for Parnell's *Hermit* and Goldsmith's *Deserted Village*. Many other cuts were done from time to time for printers in various parts of the Kingdom, these formed an almost endless variety, but at this day I have forgot both who they were for and what they were for. I engraved a series of copper plates at a low rate, for Sir Harry Liddell's and Captain Conset's Tour to Lapland in 1786. My partner and self were busily engaged about the year 1796, in engraving the plan of the projected canal from Newcastle to Carlisle for Ralph Dodd the Engineer – and plans of the estates and views of the mansion houses of a few gentlemen, who opposed the line of [the] canal on the north side of the Tyne, as projected by Mr Chapman the Engineer. After a great deal of scheming and mancuvering under the management of Ralph Heron, an attorney of great abilities, the whole *scheme* of this great, *this important national as well as local undertaking*, was baffled and set aside; and most men of disurnment were of opinion that the coal owners *below Bridge* were the cause of it. The canal, as projected by Mr Dodd, in 1795 would have certainly opened out a *territory* of coal, that might have affected their interest and it would appear, at least, that they dreaded it and in this case as in almost every other case, private interest is and was found to over power public good.

[123]

12

Having from the time that I was a school boy, been displeased with most of the cuts in children's books, and particularly with those of the 'Three hundred Animals' the figures of which, even at that time I thought I could depicture much better than those in that book; and having afterwards, very often turned the matter over in my mind, of making improvements in that publication, I at last came to the determination of commencing the attempt. The extreme interest I had always felt in the hope of administering to the pleasures and amusement of youth, and judging from the feelings I had experienced myself that they would be affected in the same way as I had been, this whetted me up and stimulated me to proceed. In this, my only reward besides, was the great pleasure I felt in imitating nature. That I would ever do any thing to attract the notice of the world, in the manner that has been done, was the farthest thing in my thoughts, and so far as I was concerned myself at that time, I minded little about any self interested considerations. These intentions, I communicated to my partner, and 'tho he did not doubt of my being able to succeed, from what he had seen of my work, yet being a prudent, cautious and thinking man, he wished to be more satisfied as to the probability of such a publication paying us for our labours. On this occasion, being little acquainted with the nature of such like undertakings, we consulted our friend Solomon Hodgson (bookseller and editor of the Newcastle Chronicle) as to the probability of its success etc, when he most warmly encouraged us to proceed. Such animals as I knew, I drew from memory upon the wood; others which I did not know, were copied from Dr Smellie's abridgement of Buffon and from other naturalists, and also from the animals which were from time to time exhibited in shows. I made sketches, first from memory, and then corrected and finished the drawings upon the wood, from a second examination of the different subjects. I begun this business of cutting the blocks, with the figure of the Dromidary on the 15 of November 1785* (the day on which my father died). I then proceeded in copying such figures (as above named) as I did not hope to see alive. The figures which were done from nature, or from memory, so much attracted the notice of our friend, that he most ardently insisted upon our making our work assume a superiour character to that of the

* November 1785 29 begun the Natural History with the figure of the Dromedary; December 2d The Camel; 10th Elephant; 12th Mufflon–Zebu; 27 Evening The Zebra.

'Shabby Book' we had been only thinking of surpassing; and from the opinion we had formed of his being better acquainted with business than we were,† we offered him a third share, free from any expense for the cuts. A proper agreament was made on the 10th of April [1790] and he became our partner in the *History of Quadrupeds*.

While I was busied in drawing and cutting the figures of the animals and also in designing and engraving the vignettes, Mr Beilby, being of a bookish or reading turn, proposed, in his evenings at home, to write or compile the descriptions, but not knowing much about natural history, we got books on that subject to enable him to form a better notion of these matters; with this, I had little more to do than in furnishing him, in many conversations and written memorandums, of what I knew of animals, and of blotting out in his manuscript what was not truth. In this way we proceeded untill the book was published in 1790. It is worthy of remark that while the title page was in hands, Mr Beilby wished to be made the author of it and wrote his name as such, 'by R Beilby' – on Mr Hodgson seeing this, without saying a word he stroked the name out with a pen, while Mr Beilby was looking on. I knew nothing about this transaction for sometime afterwards, and it might have passed so, for any thing I cared about the authorship, or whose name was put to it as such. It was sufficient for me that I had the opportunity of giving vent to my feelings and gratifying my desires in doing my part of the work. The greater part of these wood cuts were drawn and engraved at nights, after the day's work of the shop was over. In these evenings I frequently had the company of my friend and companion the Reverend Richard Oliphant who took great pleasure in seeing me work, while, at the same time, he read to me the sermons he composed for the next Sunday, where he at that time might happen to officiate. I was also often attended, from a similar curiosity, by my friend, the Reverend Thomas Hornby, Lecturer of St John's. He would not, like my friend Oliphant adjourn to a public house and join in a tankard of ale, but he had it sent for to us at my workplace. We frequently disagreed in our opinions, as to religious matters – he being, as I thought an intolerant high church-man; but notwithstanding this, he was a warm well wisher and kind friend to me – and was besides of so charitable a disposition in other respects that his purse was ever open to relieve distress and with an occasional guinea, he would commission me, anonimously, to dispose of to persons in want, and to sundry other charitable purposes.

As soon as the *History of Quadrupeds* appeared in the world, I was

† In this we were greatly mistaken, for Solomon's dissipated life prevented him attending to it.

surprized to find how rapidly the book was sold, as well as several successive editions, and this was followed by a glut of praises bestowed upon it. The first time I was obliged to hear personal praises, in this account, was from Dr David Ure LLD of Glasgow, who called to see me, and not being used to such compliments I blushed over the ears and left him talking to Mr Beilby. These and such like praises, however, excited envy, and was visibly followed by the balance of an opposite feeling from many people at home, for they raked together and blew up the embers of envy into a transient blaze; but the motives by which I was actuated stood out of the reach of its sparks, and they returned into the heap whence they came and fell into dust. I was much more affraid to meet the praises which was gathering around, than I was of the sneers which they excited, and as soon as the annexed poetry appeared in the paper, I felt obliged on its account, for sometime to shun Swarley's Club, of which George Byles* was a member, to avoid the warm and sincere compliments that awaited me there.

For the NEWCASTLE ADVERTISER.
To Mr T. BEWICK,

On his excellent Engravings on Wood, in the HISTORY
of QUADRUPEDS, published at Newcastle.

GO on great Artist in thy pleasing way,
And learn us Nature as the rising day:
Thy just Creator's wond'rous beings show,
And teach us from thy art — his boundless pow'r to know:
Thy charming pencil claims our warm applause,
And leads us on to study Nature's laws.

Though distant climes produce a savage race,
And Britain's realms present their beasts of chace,
At home we sit — peruse thy well-form'd plan,
And vindicate the ways of God to man!
Charm'd with the subject, we the theme pursue,
Nor yet forget our thanks are due to you.

Oh! at some future period may thy breast,
With other pleasing subjects be imprest:

* George Byles came from some of the southern counties and commenced school-master or teacher, in Newcastle – he had lost a leg, which probably had obliged him to take to this kind of employment, he was gentlemanly in his manners and conversation, and of a most lively and animated cast of character.

[126]

Pourtray the warbling songsters of the woods,
The scaly tribe that range the briny floods;
Depict the reptile, and the insect race,
In well-wrought lines, drawn with thy usual grace;
So shall we in this field of wonder find,
An art discover'd, and an end design'd.
                              GEO. BYLES.

I had long made up my mind, not to marry while my father and mother lived, in order that my undivided attention might be bestowed upon them. My mother, had indeed, sometime before recommended a young woman in the neighbourhood to me as a wife – she did not know the young lady intimately – but she knew she was modest in her deportment, beautiful and handsome in her person and had a good fortune. In compliance with this recommendation, I soon got acquainted and became intimate with her, but was carefull not to proceed further, and soon discovered that 'tho her character was innocence itself she was mentally one of the weakest of her sex. The smirking lasses of Tyne side had long thrown out their *jibes* against me as being a woman hater, but in this they were greatly mistaken. I had indeed been very guarded in my conduct towards them, as I held it extremely wrong and cruel to sport with the feelings of any one of them in making them believe that I was in love with any of them, without really being so; in this (which was one of my resolves) sincerity and truth were my guides – as I ever considered a matrimonial connection as a business of the utmost importance, and which was to last 'till death made the seperation. While looking about for a partner for life, my utmost attention and anxiety was directed to this important change. I had long considered it to be the duty of every man (in health) on changing his life, to get a healthy woman for his wife for the sake of his children, and a sensible one, as a companion for his own happiness and comfort. Love is the natural guide in this business, and much misery is attendant upon it, when this is awanting. This being the fixed state of my mind, I permitted no mercinary considerations to interfere. Impressed with these sentiments, I had long, my dear Jane, looked upon your mother as the most suitable inmate for me – I had seen her in prosperity and in adversity, and in the latter state she appeared to me to the greatest advantage – in this she soared above her sex, and my determination was fixed. In due time we were married and from that day to this, no cloud so far as concerned ourselves has passed over us to obscure a life time of uninterrupted happiness.

[127]

My dear 'Bell' died,
after a long and painfull illness,
on the 1st February 1826 Æ 72
(the best of wives and
very best of mothers)

During the time I was busied with the figures for the *History of Quadrupeds*, many jobs, which I have forgot, interfered to cause delay — one of which (I ought to have remembered) was the wood cut of the Chillingham Wild Bull, for the late Marmaduke Tunstal Esqr of Wycliffe. This very worthy gentleman and great naturalist, honoured me with his approbation of what I had done and was one of our correspondents. He, or my friend George Allen Esqr employed me to undertake this job — and on Easter Sunday 1789, I set off on foot to Chillingham accompanied by my acquaintance William Preston, the printer, on this business. After tarrying a little with friends at Morpeth and Alnwick, we took Huln Abbey in our way across the country to the place of our destination. Besides seeing the various kinds of pheasants etc at the last-named place, little occurred to attract attention except our being surrounded or beset (on passing a moor) amidst the fire of burning heather and afterwards passing over the surface of immense old winter wreaths of frozen snow. We took up our abode with my old kind friend John Bailey and spent a cheerfull evening with him after our fatigues, and next day he accompanied us to the park for the purpose of seeing the wild cattle. This however, did not answer my purpose, for I could make no drawing of the bull, while he, along with the rest of the herd were wheeling about and then fronting us, in the manner as described in the *History of Quadrupeds*. I was therefore obliged to endeavour to see one which had been conquered by his rival and driven to seek shelter alone in the quarry holes and in the woods — and in order to get a good look at one of this description, I was under the necessity of creeping on my hands and knees, to leward and out of his sight — and I thus got my sketch or memorandum, from which I made my drawing on the wood. I was sorry my figure was made from one before he got furnished out with his curled or shaggy neck and mane. On our return home, we took up our abode for two days and nights at Eslington, in the appartments of our kind and hearty friend John Bell, then a steward and agent to Sir Harry Liddell Bart. and afterwards a merchant at Alemouth. Having made a drawing from the large Newfoundland dog kept there — and rambling about and visiting some of Mr Bell's friends, we then bent our way homewards, highly satisfied with our journey,

[128]

The Cow's Tail or Saving the Toll

*The man has lost his hat – the cost of its replacement will be a great deal
more than the toll he is avoiding. The scene may be reminiscent of the
River Tyne at Haydon Bridge.* BM

The Titlark BM

Skating on a Frozen River ʙᴍ

Geese being carried to Market

*Jane Bewick observed that the stunted trees are a sign of the smoke-
polluted air of the nearby town.* ʙᴍ

crowned as it was with hospitality and kindness which could not be surpassed.

In the year 1790 I was employed much in the same way as I had been in other years about that period, as before noticed, but this was besides, marked with an event which enwarped and dwelt on my mind – no doubt, all thinking men in their passage through this life, must have

experienced epochs of a similar kind. My old and revered preceptor, the Reverend Christopher Gregson, died this year. No sooner did the news of his extreme illness reach my ears, than I set off, in my usual way and with all speed to Ovingham. I instantly bounced into his room, and there I found his neice, Miss Dinah Bell (afterwards Mrs Johnson) in close attendance upon him. With her, being intimately acquainted, I used no ceremony, but pulled the curtain aside and then beheld my friend in his last moments – he gave me his last look but could not speak – multitudinous reflections of things that were passed away hurried on my mind, and these overpowered me – I knew not what to say – except – farewell for ever – farewell! His sons were written to, to leave London with all speed. (I think I must have done this myself, for I cannot recollect of any person's being there at the time of their father's death – which happened that night or morning – who could undertake that office on the spurr of the moment, besides myself.)

Few men have passed away their time on Tyne side, so much respected as Mr Gregson; when he was appointed to the curacy of Ovingham, I understand his income was not more than about, thirty

[129]

pounds per annum. Thus set down, he begun by taking a few pupils to board and educate chiefly as Latin scholars, and Mrs Gregson (late Miss Langstaff) after my mother left him, did every thing in her power to make the seminary respectable. He however commenced teacher on a more extended scale by taking in scholars of all kinds from their A B C's to the Latin classes. In this, his task must have been of the most arduous and laborious description, all of which he got through without any usher or assistant. His assiduity and industry must have attracted the notice of the late Thomas Charles Bigge Esqre of Benton, the lay Rector, for he added some land to the glebe, by way of bettering his condition. Little as this farm was, as to its magnitude, it enabled him, by his good management and unceasing industry to shew himself a good farmer, and he was not a little vain on being complimented on this score. As a clergyman he was not one of the fittest for that very important office, but this was chiefly owing to his defective voice, which was so low and raucous that his hearers could not profit by his sensible discourses. In another way, I mean as a *village lawyer*, he stood preeminent – his pen was ever ready at the service of his parishioners and whatever dispute arose amongst them, there never was any objection to leave the matter to the descicion of Mr Gregson, and I have often heard it asserted, that there was not one lawsuit in the parish, while he was minister there. He set out in life, on this poor curacy, upon a system of great economy and perhaps, like other frugal people, it grew upon him 'till he was accused of nearness – but be this as it may, he accumulated a sum (as I have heard) at the time of his death, after a life of great good management, to the amount of about nine hundred pounds. If his pen was ever ready to serve his parishioners, so on certain occasions *was his purse*, for he eyed with great attention the situation, of such of his neighbours as were industrious, and when he found these were struggling under untoward circumstances or unforeseen losses, he without being solicited, lent them money to ward off the evil and to serve their nead.

The publication of the *Quadrupeds* led me into a close intimacy with Solomon Hodgson* and others of his friends, and also with other men of distinguished abilities – with Andrew Young MD, Samuel Burton Pearson MD and Nathan Surgeon, surgeon – these men were eminent in their professions and were besides of charitable humane and noble dispositions and it is equally true and distressing to think, that 'tho nature had done every thing, they, as it were, threw her favors in her face and all fell victims to *the bottle*. With this company and their

* Solomon Hodgson, the bold and independant Editor of the Newcastle Chronicle died 4 Aprill 1800 Æt 39 and was buried at St John's.

[130]

conversations, I often felt much pleased, but it sometimes led me to join with them in their excesses. There were also others with whom I occasionally spent my evenings, over a cheerfull glass in their agreable company viz – The Reverend John Hogarth (afterwards Rector of Kirknewton), my friend the Reverend Richard Oliphant, John Stokoe, architect and John Howard, the author of a work on spherical geometry. To ennumerate one half of the people with whom I was acquainted, would swell the list to an extent that might be wearysome to read over, but I may venture to name a few with whom I was in habits of intimacy and who also stood preeminent on account of their great worth and the estimation in which they were held by the public. Among the first was William Charnley, bookseller – this intelligent and honest man I account as one of the Newcastle Worthies; the Reverend William Turner, Secretary to the Literary and Philosophical Society in Newcastle and Minister of the Unitarian Chapel – he was in my way of judging a master of arts, his talents were great in various departments of science and [as a] lecturer on such subjects, and I know not how I can say more or less of him than that his character was composed of every thing, great, good, amiable and praise worthy; his friend and associate Robert Doubleday, vice President of the Literary and Philosophical Society, also partook very greatly of the same good qualities and attainments as Mr Turner. There were others, set after set, with whom I lived in habits of intimacy, and some of these may be dated a long way back – Gilfred Ward, woollen draper (of facetious memory) he died 25th of January 1798 aged 52 years and was buried at St John's; Joseph Bell, painter, he also displayed considerable abilities as a painter, poet and a man of talents in other respects – but with keeping much company he became also much dissipated – he died 26 April 1806 Æt 60 and was buried in St Andrew's; I was also long acquainted with William Bell, portrait painter etc – he was, as a painter, accounted eminent in that profession, and was awarded a gold medal, from the Society of Arts for the best Historical painting in the year. He died in Newcastle Infirmary in the year 1800 Æt 60. I was also, long afterwards on the most friendly terms, with James Ramsay, the very eminent portrait painter. Another *worthy* with whom I spent many a pleasant evening was William Gill – he had long been colliery agent to Lord Windsor (one of the partners of the Grand Allies) in which office he was much esteemed. He was a man of great reading and had reflected upon what he read; he was also, like all men of sense and spirit, of a patriotic turn, and foretold the consequences of the late war of Kings, which he considered as an attempt to destroy the civil liberties of mankind; and

[131]

I have often, since, wondered to find his predictions, unfold themselves so truely, as they have done – in this he was simple plain and argumentative and they were dictated only by truth and sincerity. He was of a social turn of mind, and for an old man was wonderfully clear, sensible and chearfull, and this prompted him to select such as he thought were of the same stamp and these he often invited to spend the evenings with him. He also, besides these pleasing qualities, was an attentively judicious and charitable man, and in this way did not do that business by halves, for wherever he found an honest man industrious, with a family struggling to get forward, he never lost sight of him, untill he placed him in a fair way to prosperity. He however outlived his faculties and left all his property past his poor relations, particularly a brother who was a poor schoolmaster, but who, I believe, he was persuaded was dead, as well as others of his near relations, whom he once intended to provide for.

13

While the sale of the *Quadrupeds* was going on, edition after edition with great success, I turned my thoughts to the *History of British Birds*. With these, I had long felt *greatly* charmed, paid great attention to, and busied myself very much in reading various descriptions or accounts of them. The first, (as far as I can now recollect) was Brookes and Miller's 'Natural History' and Dr Smellie's abridgment of Buffon – these, which were now thrown, as it were, in the background, was succeeded by Pennant's Works – first and last; I might name many others, which I had perused – chiefly lent to me by [my] kind friend George Allen Esqr – those consisted of Albin's 'History of Birds' – Belon's very old book, and 'Willughby and Ray' etc; and Mr John Rotheram* gave me Gesner's Natural History. With some of these I was in raptures – Willughby and Ray struck me as having led the way to truth and to British ornithology. The late Michael Brian Esqr† of London (formerly of Newcastle) lent me the splendid volume (planches enluminees) of Buffon, and George Silvertop Esqr of Minsteracres, Edwards' 'Natural History'. I was much pleased with 'White's History of Selborne' – Pennant's, however, opened out the largest field of information, and on his works I bestowed the most attention. Latham seems to have wound up the whole, and I have often lamented, that it was not, by being embellished with correct figures, made a great national work like the Count de Buffon's. The last of our ornithologists, and one of the most indefatigable, was the late Colonel George Montagu, author of the *Ornithological Dictionary*. As soon as it was spread abroad that we were engaged with the history of birds and their figures, I was, in consequence, led into a seemingly endless correspondence with friends and amateurs in this way, so much so, that I often felt myself unable duly to acknowledge the obligations I owed them – and many a letter I have written, after being so wearied out with the labours of the day, that I often forgot how to spell the very commonest words; and I fear the rest of many of my letters would be of a piece with this, and not clear nor very intelligible. At the beginning of this undertaking, I made up my mind to copy nothing from the works of others but to stick to nature as closely as I

* Mr John Rotheram, son of the late Dr Rotheram of Newcastle and a pupil of the good and great Linnaeus – died at [St Andrews] in the year [1804] Æ [?54].
† Michael Brian Esqr, picture dealer, London, died there on the 28 March 1821 aged 64 years.

[133]

could. And for this purpose, I was invited by Mr Constable, the then owner of Wycliffe, to visit the extensive museum there, collected by the late Marmaduke Tunstall Esqre, to make drawings of the birds. I set off from Newcastle on the 16 of July 1791 (the day on which my friend Dr Bailes died) and remained there, drawing from the stuffed specimens, nearly two months. At this beautiful place I lodged in the house of John Goundry, the person who preserved the birds for Mr Tunstall, and I boarded at his father's, George Goundry, the old miller there. While I remained at Wycliffe, I frequently dined with the Reverend Thomas Zouch, the rector of the parish – he watched my going out of the church, on the Sunday, where I often attended, accompanied by old Goundry, to invite me to dinner. On these occasions, he frequently made the characters of his late neighbour Mr Tunstall, and George Goundry, the subject of his conversation, and dwelt with great pleasure on the excellent characters of both. Mr Tunstall was a Roman Catholic and kept a chapel in his own house – Mr Zouch a Church of England Minister – and George Goundry was a Deist, and yet these three uncommonly good men, as neighbours lived in constant charity and good will towards each other. Mr Zouch would sometimes say to me, 'do you know this old man can beat me in argument' – and would then regret that he was not orthodox in his religious opinions; but setting that aside, as to his moral conduct, he was one of the best Christians he knew. Poor Goundry was equally warm in his praises of these two good men, his neighbours, and with the tear on his cheek would enumerate the charities and liberality of the late Mr Tunstall, and as a proof of the latter he instanced his being at great expense in privately contributing *very greatly* towards the pewing of Wycliffe Church. One might dwell long with pleasure on such singularly good characters – I wish the world were better stocked with them. I have often reflected with pain, on the asperity with which one description of Christians have commonly treated others who differed from them in opinion on religious matters, or rather as to their different modes of faith – and have thought that the time would come, when that cruel bloody and disgusting portion of history, would not be believed, which has recorded the facts, that one denomination of Christians actually burned others alive, who differed from them in opinion in matters which ought to have been considered as beneath contempt – but, judging from the past, it is certain that when men give up their reason, and substitute faith, or any thing else in lieu thereof, there is nothing, however absurd, that has not been believed, and no punishments, however cruel that have not been resorted to, to enforce that

[134]

belief. Men thus degraded may fairly be called *man tigers* being fitted for any wicked purpose, and under equally wicked governments they have been guided and commanded to deluge the Earth with blood. It is strange to think that this should have been the case, when it is considered that the whole of the authorities are derived from one and the same pure source, bewildered indeed by the twisted imaginations of ignorance bigotry and superstition. The inspired and benevolent Author of Christianity taught neither intolerance nor persecution. The doctrines he laid down, are plain pure and simple. They teach mercy to

the contrite, aid to the humble and eternal happiness to the good. For my own part, it is long since I left off bewildering myself with dogmas and creeds and have felt pity for those that did so – but am quite clear *and willing to believe and to allow*, that whatever modes of faith, honest and well meaning people have thought best to adopt, they might in sincerity of heart, and to the best of their judgment be doing, what is called serving God – but they surely ought not to interfere with the creeds of others who are equally as sincere, as themselves, in the means they pursue for the same ends. But however various these modes of faith may be, there is one rule that ought to guide the whole, and it appears to me simple and easy to comprehend – and that one is that all men to the utmost of their power, should endeavour through life to stear clear of every thing that may degrade their own minds and souls, that the misterious incorporated compound may not, when summonzed to leave this world, have to appear before their maker polluted and debased. The man who attends to this will fear nothing but that of erring and doing wrong – he will fear the face of no man – the little strutting authorities of despotism he will despise and the virtuous magistrate will ever be his friend – he will break no good laws that have been made for the guidance of man in society, and as to his religion, that is an affair between himself and his maker only – with the Author of his being, he will with unentangled mind commune freely at all times, when his spirit moves him to do so – and no man ever did, or ever will feel himself happy, that does not pursue this course through life.

Ever since I habituated myself to think, I have always seen, as clearly as I could see any thing, that it is the intention of the Deity that mankind should live in a state of civilized society and that no period of human existence can be comfortable without the pleasures and endearments of social intercourse. Every object in nature that can be contemplated upon shews this, and the full and exact fitness of all its component parts clearly prove that man from his social nature is destined to live in this state. He has been endowed with reason, as his guide for the purpose of regulating and conducting the whole, but when that guide is neglected and he suffers his selfish propensities and bad passions to mislead him from the path of rectitude, from that moment every thing, so far as this reaches, goes wrong. For reasons of this kind, it is necessary that equitable and just laws should be made and inforced, to restrain vice from breaking down the barriers that are erected to protect virtue and patriotism – and to break through these laws is sin. But in the present wretched state of society, it may be difficult to bring about such a reformation of manners, as would ensure the accomplishment of so desirable an end, for it appears to me that the character of mankind ought to be new modelled before this can be effectually done.

Having long busied myself in wading through systems on natural history, its orders, genera, species and varieties, the whim has often struck me to lay down an imaginary one, of classing mankind – the Genus Homo may be made to consist of three species and their varieties – the first (including in one the wise and good) is honest men, the second is knaves and the third fools – these and their gradations and varieties gliding into each other, form the present jumbled mass of society – the community of which we all form a part. As any of these may happen to predominate in the government of society, so in exact proportion will the good, bad and indifferent effects of their management be felt by the whole people. I think it will be admitted that out of the first species ought to be chosen every man, according to his mental powers and the education he may have received to call forth these powers, to enable him to fill every public office from the constable up to the king – out of the two latter species, when conjoined, are formed the great mass of the wicked, gross, vulgar herd (high and low) of mankind. Among these, knaves of great abilities ought to be particularly guarded against. They are a kind of splendid devils, who have from time immemorial spread abroad much misery in the world – but

[136]

notwithstanding their abilities they would not have got forward in their public wickedness, nor have formed their majorities without enlisting, as tools, their ready made auxiliaries the fools. And if we take only a slight glance at individual misery it will be seen that most of it is inflicted by one man upon another: 'man's inhumanity to man makes countless thousands mourn'. Could this be remedied, what a beautifull world would this appear to thousands, instead of being obliged thus to view it through the medium of an almost perpetual cheerless gloom.

I have often amused myself in considering the character of the canine species, and of comparing it and its varieties with those of the untutored part of mankind, and it is curious and amusing to see the similarity between them – to his master the dog is an uncommonly submissive, obedient and faithfull servant, and seems to look upon him as if he were

an angel – his sagacity and his courage are equally conspicuous, and in the defence of his master he will suffer death. But to his own species he is ill behaved, selfish, cruel and unjust; he only associates with his fellows for the purpose of packing together to destroy other animals, which cannot be effected otherwise. They will sometimes indeed let a supplicating dog, into which they have inspired terror, sneak off, and I have often watched to see the wary circumspect plan that a strange dog adopts on his being obliged to pass through a village, or through among those of their equally ill behaved brethren, the butchers' dogs, in a town – it is curious to see the stranger, upon these occasions view his danger and then to affect lameness and go hirpling through amongst them unmolested. I knew their instinct was surprizing, but to know some of their reasoning powers I had not tried, and for this purpose, when a boy, I cut two thin slices of meat and plastered the insides with mustard, and then threw it to one of my father's dogs. This, he being very very

[137]

apt at kepping, caught in his mouth, and as quickly as he could, got quit of it again, but from that time, he would rather run the risk of losing it, than kep any more. And to prove how far selfishness and malignity would operate upon him – I have placed two basons filled with very hot fat broth, at a distance from each other – he ran from one to the other, to prevent a beautiful spaniel bitch, from partaking of either of them. His attention was taken up with thus watching and preventing her, 'till at length his patience was exhausted by going so often from one bason to the other, and then, with the utmost vengeance he seized her and tore away his mouthfull of skin from her side.

On my return from Wycliffe, being thoroughly drenched with an incessant rain, I called upon my old and much valued schoolfellow, John Forster, at Bishop Auckland, and spent a day or two with him in busy converse about our former transactions at school etc. Perhaps few have passed through life without experiencing the pleasure that a retrospect of the times passed thus afford to old cronies, in talking over the recollections of youthfull frolics and even the disipline which followd in consequence of them. As soon as I arrived in Newcastle, I immediately began to engrave from the drawings of the birds I had made at Wycliffe, but I had not been long thus engaged 'till I found the very great difference between preserved specimens and those from nature, no regard having been paid at that time to place the former in their proper attitudes, nor to place the different series of the feathers, so as to fall properly upon each other. This has always given me a great deal of trouble to get at the markings of the dishevelled plumage, and when done with every pains, I never felt satisfied with them. I was on this account driven to wait for birds newly shot, or brought to me alive, and in the intervals employed my time in designing and engraving tail pieces or vignettes. My sporting friends however supplied me with birds as fast as they could, but none more so than my kind friend Lt Henry Forster Gibson of the fourth Dragoons, Lt Col. Dalton, Major Shore, Capt. Dalbiac (now General Dalbiac) and other officers of the same Regiment also shewed great attention to our growing work. George Strickland Esqr of Ripon also interested himself in his contributions for the same end. Besides these many birds were sent to me from various parts of the kingdom but the obligations I owed to these are mostly acknowledged in their proper place in the work. After working many a late hour upon the cuts, the first volume of the book was, at length, finished at press in September 1797. Our friend Solomon Hodgson, had no share with us in this work. Mr Beilby undertook the writing or compilation of this (the first) volume, in which I assisted him

[138]

a great deal more than I had done with the *Quadrupeds*. I was however surprized to find, that in an Introduction written by him in which he took occasion to bestow the most unqualified praises upon me, for the assistance I had given him, by which I found he was this time determined upon being an author. I only observed that I thought the *Quadrupeds*, with the title of 'Beilby and Bewick' as the editors had done very well and I could see no reason for making any change. I found Mr Beilby had imparted his intentions of becoming author to the Reverend Thomas Hornby, while the latter was at supper with him, as indeed he often was, when Mr Hornby took occasion to express his opinion of the business and to advise him not to think upon doing any such thing, observing that he could have written a history of birds for me, and that some of the doctors I was so intimate with, would with pleasure have done the same, perhaps better than he could have done it, but that in neither case could they have hoped to sell a single edition without my cuts. After Mr Hornby had slept and turned the business over in his mind, he called upon me and with a kind of indignant feeling advised me not to permit any such thing; other friends also did the same and used the same kind of reasoning. In this unsettled state of our affairs, Mr and Mrs Beilby set off in the pet, upon a visit to Mr Wilkinson's at Sleekburn, where they remained about a fortnight. On Mr Beilby's return, I asked him if he still persisted in being named as the author of the book to which he replied in the affermative. 'Then, Sir,' said I, 'if you can point out any single sentence, from one end of this volume of the *History of Birds* to the other, of original matter as your own, I shall be glad to see it' – at this he hesitated. I then proposed to him to leave the discussion, as to the authorship to our mutual friends, who knew every thing relative to the matter in dispute between us, adding that if they agreed in thinking that he ought to be 'the author' it should be so, and that I never would say a word more about it. To this he agreed, and as the work was at a stand, no time was to be lost – after naming our referees. Mr Charnley, the Reverend William Turner, Mr Solomon Hodgson and Mr Robert Doubleday were instantly for that purpose summonzed to meet that afternoon. We both guessed, without saying a word to each other, that Mr Charnley would be fixed upon as President, and he being very deaf, we each of us, without mentioning our intentions, stated our seperate cases in writing directed to him. As soon as he and his collegues had read Mr Beilby's he handed it to me and I read it; mine was next given to Mr Charnley who in like manner shewed it to the others and then gave it to Mr Beilby, but he declined looking at it and it was given to me again. After this we were desired to retire, when

[139]

they committed what they had agreed upon to writing, the whole of which was printed in the concluding part of the preface to the first volume of the *Birds*. And so the matter was left, without naming either him or myself as authors of the work, otherwise than as before, and of the wood cuts being acknowledged as my own. After this Mr Beilby

gave up the engraving business and dedicated his whole time to the watch cristal and clock manufactory, in which he had been long engaged before our seperation.

The printing of other editions of the first volume of the *Birds* still met with a ready sale – but some disputes happening between us and Mrs Hodgson, the widow of our much esteemed friend, respecting the printing of the *Quadrupeds* – Mr Beilby who now sought repose, and could not be turmoiled with disputes of any kind, sold me his third share of that publication. Sometime before the second volume of the *Birds* was put to press, he also sold me his half share of this first volume. For his third share of the *Quadrupeds* I paid him one hundred pounds, and for his half share of the first volume of the *Birds*, I paid him *three hundred pounds*. I had no sooner agreed to give this latter sum, than many recollections of the past crouded upon my mind, and looking at the unfavourable side, I could not help thinking of the extra labour and time I had spent in the completion of these works, wherein he bore comparatively a small part, nor even an equivelent as to his time and labour in the other department of our business, and in this instance I could not help thinking that he had forgot himself and had suffered greadiness to take possession of his mind; but having promised to pay this sum I made no further observations about it, to any one. On the other side of this account, I called to my remembrance the many obligations I owed him for the wise admonitions he had given and the example he had set me, while I was only a wild and giddy youth – these I never could forget and they implanted so routed a respect for him that I had grudged nothing I could do to promote his happiness. I noticed, for sometime past, that he had been led, under a guidance and influence, that made an alteration in his conduct and character for the worse and he appeared to me not to be the *Ralph Beilby** he had been, for before this he deservedly bore the character of being a sensible, judicious, fair dealing and industrious man, and a good member of society. I used always to think him carefull and sometimes near and this disposition might indeed have crept and increased upon him – but whatever natural failings might be in his composition, these had hither-tofore been checked and regulated by the rules of morality and religion. It seemed to me that it must have been a maxim with him to do justice to all, but not to confer favors upon any one – and yet he often joined me in conferring such in various ways, upon our apprentices and other of our work people, for which we commonly had dirt thrown in our faces. It does not require any great stretch of observation, to discover that gratitude is a rare virtue and that whatever favors are poured upon an ungratefull man, he will conclude that these favors would not have been bestowed upon him had he not deserved them. In these our gifts to 'prentices and others of that stamp, I was to blame in thus conferring our favors that it would have been as well to let alone. In other charities he was not backward in contributing his mite, but in these matters he was led by wisdom – in the former case – mine, by giving vent to my feelings, was led by folly – but indeed these follies were trivial compared with others relative to money matters, in which I had also given vent to my feelings, in lending money to some and in being bound for the payment of it, for others – in which, if I had been more of his dis-position would not have happened, and I now clearly see and feel had it not been for these imprudencies, I should at this day, have found myself in better and very different circumstances from those I am in – my partner indeed often watched and sometimes prevented me from engaging in such ruinous concerns – and would remark to me that it was impossible to serve any man who would not serve himself.

After Mr Beilby was done with any concern in the publications, I found I could not go on pleasantly with Mrs Hodgson in the printing of the *Quadrupeds*, and I therefore offered, either to buy her share or sell her mine, but this she declined doing and sometime after this, she sold hers to Messrs Longman & Co London – and since that time, the publication, shared in this way, has gone on between us.

* Ralph Beilby, engraver, Newcastle, died 4 of January 1817 Æt 74 and was buried at St Andrew's.

As soon as Mr Beilby left me, I was obliged from necessity – not choice, to commence author. As soon as each bird was finished on the wood, I set about describing it from my specimen – and at the same time consulted every authority I could meet with to know what had been said, and this together with what I knew from my own knowledge, were then compared, and in this way, I finished, as truely as I could, the second volume of the *History of British Birds*. I also examined the first volume with a view to correct its errors, and also to add many new figures and descriptions of them to it. Although all this of thus taking the whole upon me, could not be done, but by close and indeed severe confinement and application, yet I was supported under these by the extreme pleasure I felt in depicturing and describing these beautiful and very interesting aireal wanderers of the British Isles. I also hoped that my labours might perhaps have the effect of inveigling my youthfull countrymen, as far as I could, to be smitten with the charms which this branch – and indeed every other department of natural history imparts, and these endless pleasures they afford to all who wish to trace nature up to Nature's God.

While I was thus proceeding, I was countenanced, encouraged and flattered by amateurs who took a deep interest in my growing work and seemed to partake of the ardour in which I had long indulged myself – from them birds were sent to me both far and near – but to give a list of the names of those friends, and to detail the kindness I experienced first and last, might indeed be giving vent to my feelings of gratitude but it would far exceed the bounds prescribed to this memoir.

14

While I was engaged with the figures of the Water Birds and the vignettes, and writing the history, this business was greatly retarded by my being obliged often to lay that work aside and to do various other jobs in the wood engraving, and also the work of the shop for my customers in the town, but particularly, writing engraving, which I may say I was obliged to learn and to pursue after Mr Beilby left me, and the most interesting part of this kind of work, was plates for bank notes, checks etc. As one of the most important of these was a 5£ note for the Carlisle Bank, which attracted much notice, it may be right to give some account of it. It happened one evening while I was in company with George Losh Esqr who was some way connected with that Bank, he asked me if I could engrave a note that could not easily be forged. In reply I told him I thought I could. 'Then,' said he, 'do it immediately,' and I lost no time in beginning upon it. I had at that time never seen a ruling machine, nor the beautifull engine turning lately brought into use by Perkins, Fairman and Heath, which was at that time (I believe) utterly unknown. I however proceeded with my plate and my object was to make the device look like a wood cut, and in this ('tho a first attempt) I succeeded and the number of impressions wanted were sent to Carlisle. Not long after this, I was told by Sir T[homas] F[rankland] Bart, that his brother, who held some office under Government, and who was in the habit of being much with the late King George III, whose curiosity was insatiable as to every thing relative to the arts, had got one of these bank notes and greatly admired and approved of it. About two years after this (in the year [1801]) Samuel Thornton Esqr of the Bank of England, wrote to me respecting this note, and wished to know how it was done and whether it was executed on wood or on copper etc. I was strongly advised by a friend not to give the gentlemen of that bank, any information whatever about my plate, for, said he, as soon as they know the nature of what they are enquiring after, you will hear no more from them. I did not take his advice, and after a deal of trouble in writing to them and stating, among many other matters, that 'tho my plate would do well for country banks, it would not do for the great number wanted for the Bank of England. So the business ended in nothing, and I heard no more from them. It may perhaps be well, while I am on the subject of bank notes to pass over a number of years, and come down to the year [1818] when a Commission was appointed to

[143]

investigate the business of forgeries and to endeavour to prevent them in future. But sometime previous to this, I was employed by my friend John Bailey Esqr of Chillingham, to engrave plates to prevent the *pen and ink* forgeries which had been committed upon the Berwick Bank, which it was found had been better imitations than could be made from copper plates. In this I succeeded; and also (by a simple process) on the plates for the Northumberland Bank.

Immediately on the heel of this, and as soon as the Commissioners, above mentioned commenced their enquiries, it seemed as if the services and abilities of all the artists in the kingdom were held in requisition, to give in their specimens and their schemes for this purpose; and, willing to contribute all in my power to accomplish so desirable an end, I among many others gave in my plan. The leading objects with me were perminancy, or in other words to aim at executing a device that would *never* nead either alteration or repairs; and the other part of my plan, was that the device should be of such a nature that all men of common discernment could easily recognise the note as a legitimate one. I did not mention, in my letters to Sir Joseph Banks, any thing about using types or how highly I approved of their use, because I believed that others had done so before; to point out in which way I conceive they would have been of great importance, would now be useless, since the Commissioners or the Bank, have rejected every scheme (so far as I know) that had been laid before them. This to me always appeared strange, since in my opinion there has been several specimens laid before them perfectly efficient for the purpose of preventing forgeries, or perhaps totally setting that nefarious work at rest. The beautifull specimens first produced by Perkins, Fairman and Heath from their steel plates or blocks, were in my opinion inimitable and quite sufficient to answer the end intended, and those afterwards brought forward under the auspices of Sir William Congreve are nearly of the same character and import. If an engine turner cannot set his lathe, so as to trace or copy the same delicate and truely exact curves and lines etc which are shewn in both, it is not likely that any forgery will ever be attempted upon either of them; if they had been less complex, I would have liked them better – but as they are, the best engravers on either copper, steel or wood, will not attempt an imitation – they may indeed gaze at them – *but that is all*. It was always surprizing to me, that none of the ingenious schemes, so long under the consideration of the Commissioners were not adopted; but when I read, in a newspaper, that Mr Pierce had stood up in the House of Commons, and in answer to some questions put to him there, said in reply, 'that the Commissioners

The Tawny Owl B M

The Skylark I B

The Little Bittern B M

The Blackbird B M

were of opinion *that nothing better than the old Bank note could be devised to prevent forgery*!!!' then indeed, on reading this, I could scarcely believe my own eyes – my astonishment was complete – and my opinion of the whole business of this mountain in labour was fixed.

During the time that the business of the Commissioners seemed to me to be hanging in suspense, I wrote a letter to Sir Joseph Banks, in which I endeavoured to press upon the attention of him and the rest of his colleagues, the necessity of having the blank paper of country bank notes, printed with whatever new device they might have approved of to prevent forgery, instead of the little duty stamp, used by Government, which had only the duty in view. Sometime after this, a long account of the invention of Sir William Congreve Bart, was published in the *Repository of Arts* in March 1822, setting forth how much country bankers and the whole country was obliged to him, as the inventor of, or the person who first suggested this scheme so essentially important to them, as that of preventing forgeries upon their banks. As soon as I had read this, I answered it in the *Monthly Magazine* of May 1822 in which I quoted my letters to the Commissioners, with the dates, bearing upon this very subject, and claiming the priority of my suggestions to them; at the same time I only requested Sir William Congreve, would on the word of a gentleman, say whether or not this suggestion was his or mine. Of this neither Sir William nor any of the Commissioners took any notice – excepting indeed, something *purporting to be an answer* to what I had said, by a person in the employ of Sir William as an artist, which 'tho it begun very impudently, did not answer my letter at all. This I could not help treating with contempt, and to enter into something like a paper war with such a person I thought would be great folly. Sir William appears to be going on prosperously by furnishing bankers with his stamped notepapers and printing them in the way above described. Sir William, as a Commissioner, had the opportunity and advantage of seeing the various devices and knowing the opinions of the various artists upon these devices, which enabled him to cull and select such as appeared to him best calculated to prevent forgery; and, as he was no artist himself, I think he should not have taken any of the credit to himself, either as the inventor or executor of any of these specimens – nor have turned the profit arising from them to his own private account.

Long before the Commissioners were appointed to investigate the business of forgeries, I got engaged in another work, on my own account.

15

During a severe illness, with which I was visited in April 1812, brought on by a violent perspiration suddenly checked – the particulars of which I nead not detail to my dear Jane, as the part you and your mother and sisters took to nurse me night and day, for so long a time, must be fresh in all your memories, I determined, if I did recover, to go on with a publication of *Esop's Fables*. While I lay helpless from weakness and pined to a skeleton, without any hopes of a recovery being entertained either by myself, or any one else, I became, as it were, all mind and memory; I readily had presented to my recollection almost every thing that had passed through life, both of what I had done and what I had left undone, and at last, when after much debating in my own mind where I should be buried, I fixed upon Ovingham; and when this was settled, I became quite resigned to the will of omnipotence and felt happy. I could not however help regretting that I had not published a book, similar to Croxall's *Esop's Fables*, as I had always intended to do. I was always extremely fond of that book, and as it had afforded me much pleasure, I thought with better executed designs, it would impart the same kind of delight to others that I had experienced from attentively reading it. I was also of opinion that it had in the same way, while admiring the cuts, led hundreds of young men into the paths of wisdom and rectitude, and perhaps in that way had done more good than the pulpit. As soon as I was so far recovered as to be able to sit at the window at home, I immediately begun to draw designs upon the wood, of the fables and vignettes, and to me this was a most delightfull task. In impatiently pushing forward to get to press with the publication, I availed myself of the help of my pupils, (my son, William Harvey and William Temple) who were also eager to do their utmost to forward me in the engraving business and in my struggles to get the book ushered into the world. Notwithstanding the pleasurable business of bringing out this publication, I felt it also an arduous undertaking. The execution of the fine work of the cuts, during the day light, was very trying to the eyes, and the compiling or writing the book by candle light in my evenings at home, together injured the optic nerve and that put the rest of the nerves *out of tune*, so that I was obliged for a short time, to leave off this intense application untill I somewhat recovered the proper tone of memory and sight again. I found in this book more difficulties to conquer than I had experienced with either the *Quadrupeds*

[146]

or the *Birds*. The book was finished at press on the 1st October 1818 and was not so well printed as I expected and wished – the ink for such fine work being much too strong, black and thick. I am pleased to find the second edition, December 1823, better printed and better managed in other respects.

(*Thus far from page 101 [p. 114 of this book] was written, during my stay in Tynemouth which I left on the 22 December 1823.*)

During the eventful period of the French Revolution, and the wide spreading war which followed in consequence of it, and in which our Government became deeply engaged and commenced its war operations in 1793 and continued 'till the peace of 1814 – a life time of blood and slaughter – I frequently, by way of unbending the mind after the labours of the day, spent my evenings (chiefly at the Blue Bell) in company with a set of staunch advocates for the liberties of mankind, who discussed the passing events mostly with the cool, sensible and deliberate attention, which the importance of the subject drew forth. I have already before named some of these acquaintances, to which I may now add some others, forming altogether a missellaneous group, but over whom some men of sense and consequence in Newcastle who were commonly of the party, and from their superiour attainments seemed to preside to set the example of propriety of conduct to those of a more violent turn of mind; but indeed the political enormities of the times excited the indignation of many, which it was not easy to keep within due bounds. The parties which frequented the Blue Bell, and the News Room there, consisted of tradesmen, bankers' clerks, artizans and agents of various kinds. But those with whom I particularly associated there were Ralph Crawford, shoe maker, Joseph Bulmer, builder, Phineas Crowther, founder, Michael Charlton, white smith, John Mitchell, editor of the *Tyne Mercury*, Count Raymond, French teacher and fencing master, and my more constant companion, David Sivright, gentleman was a man of extraordinary abilities and attainments – he belonged to an opulent family near Edinburgh, had been brought up to business in a bank there, and was afterwards a wine merchant in London, where he had associated with the highest ranks of society. I believe he failed, or at least did not prosper in business. He had been in the West Indies, and returned home in a merchant ship, in company with Rodney's fleet and the French ships of war, his prizes, of which so remarkable a destruction took place in the great storm they had to encounter on their voyage to England. Whether he had been a disappointed man in the world, I know not, but to me he appeared so; he had

[147]

a routed bad opinion of most of the people in very high life – with respect to whom he might be called a misanthropist; but to others he was affable and kind, and felt most poignantly for the distress of the unfortunate and was ever ready to relieve them. Against the former description he appeared to me to be too violent; to the latter I think he shewed something of a sickly sensibility. He could make himself extremely pleasant in company he liked, but to such as he thought badly of either as fools or knaves (and in this he was whimsical), with them he became quite outrageous. I think I was the last person he associated with and even with me he often shewed petulant, and as often apologized for it. He had long been used to wander about alone and took to drinking to excess. He left Newcastle and went to Blyth where he died, aged 68.

I sometimes dropped in upon other parties of friends of various political opinions and attainments, at Mrs Jane Elliot's,* at the Sign of the Unicorn. These were mostly tradesmen of the genteel sort, and besides them, this house had been a kind of rendezvous, or house of resort to the comedians of our Theatre during the season for many years back, from the time of Heaton & Austin's Company, down to those conducted by Charles Whitlock, Joseph Munden, Stephen Kemble etc, and still later, comprising a period of the times of Massey and Jeffries, Plat, Emery, Cook, Liston and many others who made a figure in their day. With Joseph Munden I often associated, and still oftener and to a later period with my friend Stephen Kemble and his friends. In her house and indeed in every house, politics formed the topic of conversation, and less or more, for years back, seemed the order of the day.

In my partaking in these debatings, I now find I spent rather too much time. I fear it was useless – for it requires little descernment to see that where a man's interest is at stake he is very unwilling to hear any argument that militates against it, and people who were well paid, were always very loyal. To argue on any subject, unless a principle, or what mathemeticians would call a datum, is first laid down to go upon, the conversation is only gabble. It begins and must end in nonsense; and I suspect that many of the long wearisome speeches and debatings, for such a number of years, in the House of Lords and Commons, as well as many of the innumerable weekly or dayly essays and some of the

* Jane Elliot, as a landlady, conducted herself with great propriety. She was sensible, spirited, clever and obliging and from these qualifications and from her handsome and majestic appearance, was called the Queen of Landladies. She died 12 October 1822 Æ 74 and was buried at St John's and on the same day, with her friend Mrs Sarah Hodgson the widow of Solomon Hodgson.

pamphlets which the revolution and the war gave rise to, were very often carried on without laying down a right principle – a principle of rectitude, to guide them. But the causes of this horrid Revolution and the equally horrible war which ended it, will form a most interesting subject for the head and the pen of some future historian of a bold and an enlightened mind, truely to depicture it in all its bearings – long after the animosity of party feelings and the parties themselves have died away.

From the best consideration I have been able to give the question on this momentous dispute, I cannot help viewing it otherwise than in this way. In the year 1789 the French Revolution broke out first of all from the income of the Government not being sufficient to defray its expenditures, or in other words, from its finances having become deranged for want of money – and which the people, having been taxed to the utmost and brought down to poverty could no longer supply. The aristocracy and the priesthood (the priviledged orders as they were called) contributed little or nothing to support the state, and they quite forgot, that instead of their being the natural guardians, or depositories of the honour and virtue to the nation, they were chiefly known only as its oppressors, and their exactions and their cruelties and tyrany by which the people had long been born down to the lowest pitch of degradation, and were long considered not as rational human beings, equal in mind and intellect to themselves, but as beings made for the purpose only of continually labouring, to support them in all their real and imaginary wants, and then to be treated worse than beasts of burthen. This is nearly the case in all countries where such numbers of the aristocracy are kept up, blinded by misplaced pride and guided by ignorance; and these again have what may be called their satellites – a kind of bastard breed, who in aping the worst part of the character of those exalted above them, shewed themselves off as the opulent, aspiring, purse proud gentry of a country.

> *If aught on earth the immortal powers deride,*
> *'Tis surely this, – the littleness of pride.*

This kind of treatment, so long shewn to the people of France could be endured no longer; they indeed seemed heartily disposed and would have settled a rational and just representative Government, quietly enough themselves, but this did not suit the views of the surrounding despots, to whom the very word liberty, was offensive to their ears – it was terrible, and not to be listned to for a moment – and it was determined at once, that this attempt of that people to resume their

[149]

rights, should instantly be overwhelmed and crushed at once, and for this purpose, their immense [numbers of] armed, well deciplin'd mercinaries, were gathered together and almost surrounded the country. Thus situated, and remembering the traditionnary tales handed down to them, of the cruelties and oppressions under which their forefathers had groaned, the French people could not bear the thoughts of it any longer – they were driven to madness, and instantly retaliated those long matured enormities, upon those who they conceived meant, in like manner, that they and their children's children should continue to be doomed to bear the same for ages to come. In this state of the public mind, the French people rose simultaneously, as one man, and with unconquerable energy and bravery, like a whirlwind swept off the advocates and the armies of despotism in heaps, or one after another, from the face of the earth. Thus roused, this confedracy of Legitimates, finding or fearing that they might be baffled in their attempts, it would appear, looked to England for support; and grieved indeed were the advocates for rational liberty and well wishers to their country, to find that the enemies of freedom had not looked in vain – for the Government, the Government of this free country! and free people! – long veering indeed from the right line of rectitude *and freedom* had readily found pretexts for bending it to aside, that it might be the more easily broken when the fit opportunity presented itself; and pretexts and pretences were also as readily found for entering into this war of despotism, and war was begun in the year 1793 against the then Republican Government of France. It had long been the settled opinion of many profound politicians, that corruption had spread and was spreading its baneful influence among the members of the Government of this kingdom, and that the majority of them cared nothing about maintaining the constitution in its purity, which to them was become like an old song. In this state of things and ready primed, with Mr Pitt at their head and the resources of the British Isles in his hands, it was calculated upon as a certainty that this weight added to the already powerfull confedracy, would soon put a stop to the march of intellect, and if found necessary, put an extinguisher upon the rights of man. It is horrible to contemplate the immense destruction of human beings and the waste of treasure which supported and followed this superlatively wicked war. Under the mask of patriotism, Mr Pitt had begun his career, but he soon changed sides and (blinded perhaps by ambition) became the powerfull advocate of an opposite and perverted order of things. Thus situated, nothing could to a certainty serve his purpose so well, as corruption, and the House of Commons had long been growing

[150]

into a state befitting them for this purpose, for they had in a great degree ceased to be the representatives of the people; and he had now only to begin an invigorated, new, or more extended system of place and patronage, to have the majority of the House at his nod, and in aid of this to add an extension of the peerage. This demi oligarchy, cemented together by the same fellow feeling of rapacious interests thus set agoing, this British government, in his hands was at once the best organised system of extorting money ever acted upon to fleece their sub-

jects that had appeared in the world. They then met together to tax – tax – tax and under various pretexts to rob the people 'according to law' and to divide the spoil among themselves and their friends. They passed arbitrary laws, gagging bills were passed, and a system of espionage spread over the whole kingdom, to keep the people down, many of whom seemed to have forgotten the exertions of their forefathers whose blood had been spilt to purchase a better order of things. I felt particularly hurt at the apathy of country gentlemen, in these (politically considered) worst of times; their faculties seemed benumbed – but indeed most of them fell into the vortex of corruption themselves. They appeared to me to have lost their former independant character and to be now looking out to that evil source as a provision for the younger branches of their own families, unmindfull of all other ill consequences which this selfishness blindly supported and maintained. The minions of power, and spies, were countenanced and protected, by which they became insolent and impudent and walked in stately array hand in hand in safety. Altho the friends of liberty and the constitution in its purity, were both numerous and intrepid, yet for want of what they termed respectable heads, they were widely spread and divided, and their efforts proved in vain. There was also an intermediate or kind of nutral race, of those who had not laid down any principle in politics to guide them; they were mostly such as advocated the cause of corruption, and in listning to them, I was often disgusted at their senseless arguments; they were proof against reasoning and thoroughly convinced me that a wise man changes his opinion, but a fool never does. They however kept on the safe side – they *were loyal*, and the jist of their arguments with which they ended all their disputes, were summed up in this – 'if you do not *like your Country* leave it – What do you want? are not *we* very well off?' – their reflecting powers reached no further, and they could not see the slow degrees by which the arm of despotism had so often circumspectly stretched its iron hand over the liberties of the people and then crushed them. While bickerings and debatings were going on among politicians at home, the Continent was deluged with the blood of many destructive battles. The sea was also stained with it in the same way, and it was on this element that the tide of affairs was first turned in favour of Britain, who now by the valour of her seamen reigned complete 'mistress of the deep', and the commerce of the world seemed to be poured into her lap. Estates rose in value to an extraordinary height and the price of grain etc still more so in proportion. The shipping interest wallowed in riches; the gentry whirled about in aristocratic pomposity; they forgot what their demeanour and good, kind, behaviour, used to be to those of inferiour stations in life and seemed now, far too often, to look upon them like dirt. The character of the farmers, was also *totally* altered, from what it used to be, and they now acted the gentleman very awkwardly; they could not, in these times, drink any thing but wine, and even that was called 'humble port', and they were to have such kinds as bore a higher price. When they left the market, they were fitted to ride over all they met or overtook on the way. But this was as nothing compared to the pride and folly which took possession of their empty, or fume charged heads, when they got dressed in scarlet – they were then fitted for any purpose and were called '*Yeomanry Cavelry*' – pride and folly in them then became personified. When peace came, it brought with it a sudden fall of the prices of corn; but the taxes continuing the same to them, and rents still keeping high, they (with few exceptions) suddenly experienced a woefull change. I cannot say, after seeing so much of their folly, that I was sorry for them, for they mostly deserved this reverse of fortune. Not so with the industrious labourer: his privations were great and he was undeservedly doomed to suffer for want of employment and often to waste away and die of hunger and want.

During the war, the landholders may be said to have paid little or nothing to support it, for their extra rents paid almost all their taxes; at length the evils brought on by so long a war, fell also heavily upon numbers of them who, on account of tythes and taxes, with which the land was loaded, they could hardly get any rent at all. It will seem a wonder to future ages, how the British people could so long support the squandered expenditure of the Government – but they are still not like the long-worn-down subjects of continental despots – for what they can get from their subjects is like clipping the fleece from the back and sides of swine – while the ingenuity, the industry and the energy of the British people furnish the well grown fleeces of sheep, and it is a great pity they should have been so often wickedly fleeced to the bare skin.

This state of temporary internal prosperity first excited to agricultural improvements, and societies for the promotion and premiums for the encouragement of its various desiderata, blazed forth over [a] great part of the kingdom – cattle, sheep, horses and swine – all of which was called 'live stock', occupied *a great deal* of their attention and in the improvement of the various breeds they surely succeeded to [a] certain extent – and in some cases, perhaps to a great extent, and yet I cannot help thinking that they often suffered their whimsies to overshoot the mark and in many instances, to lead them on to the *rediculous*. But after all these enquiries, evil it seems, must be mixed with good in this life, for the eyes of the landlords were so opened to their own interest, in what was made apparent, that the man of industry, the plain plodding farmer, did and will have to pay for these improvements.

My kind – my intimate – my old friend, John Bailey Esqre of Chillingham, in conjunction with another friend of mine, George Cully Esqr of Fowberry, were the active, judicious and sensible authors of many of the agricultural reports in which they did not lose sight of the farmer, and they wished to inculcate the principle 'to live and let live', between the landlord and his tenant.

It will readily be supposed, that where such exertions were used, and pains taken to breed the best kinds of all the domestic animals, that jealousy and envy would be excited, and contentions arise as to which were the best – but for me to dilate upon this, would only lead me out of my way. I shall however notice an instance, as it happened to be between my two friends Mr Smith, of Woodhall and Mr Bailey. The latter, in his report of the Cheviot sheep, had given a bad figure of a ram of that breed. This was construed into a design to lessen the character of Mr Smith's Cheviot sheep, on which occasion, in April 1798, Mr Smith sent for me to make a drawing of one of his rams, to be engraved – partly by way of contrasting it with the figure Mr Bailey had done in the same way for his report. The colour Mr Smith gave to the business was not to find fault with Mr Bailey's figure, but to shew how much Mr Smith had improved the breed since Mr Bailey had written his report, and given his figure along with it. While I was at Woodhall I was struck with the sagacity of one of Mr Smith's shepherd's dogs – that part of their character was well known – but this was exemplified *before my own eyes*. Mr Smith wished to have a particular ram brought out from among the flock, for the purpose of my seeing it. Before we set out, he observed to the shepherds, that he thought the old dog (he was grey headed and almost deaf and blind) would do well enough for what he wanted with him. Before we reached the down where the flock was feeding, I observed Mr Smith was talking to the dog before he ordered him off on this errand; and while we were talking on some indifferent subject, the dog brought a ram before us, upon which Mr Smith found a deal of fault with the dog – 'did I not order you so and so?' and scolded him, as if he had been a man, for bringing a wrong one. He then set him off again to bring the ram he wished to see – this was then soon done, and the other animal was suffered again to join the flock. After fresh directions had been given, we then returned home and shortly after our arrival there, the dog brought the very ram wanted, along with a few of the sheep, into the fold, where I took the drawing of him.

Shortly after my return home from Woodhall, I was sent for to go to Darlington and thence to Barmpton, to make drawings of cattle and sheep to be engraved for a Durham report. After I had made my drawings, I soon saw that such as I had made from the fat sheep, were not such as were wanted, but these were to be made like the *such and such* paintings as were shewn to me. I observed that these paintings were nothing like the animals whose figures I had made my drawings from, and that I would not alter mine to suit the paintings that were shewn to me, nor put my name to such; but if it were wished that I should make engravings from these paintings, I had not the slightest objection to do so, and that I would also endeavour to make fac similies of them – but this proposal would not do, and my journey, as far as concerned these fat-cattle makers, ended in nothing. I would not put lumps of fat here and there to please them where I could not see it – at least [not] in so exagerated a way as on the painting before me – so I got my 'labour for my trouble'. Many of the animals were, during *this rage* for fat cattle, surely fed up to as great a weight and bulk as it was possible for feeding to make them, but this was not enough, they were to be figured monstrously fat before the owners of them could be pleased. Some painters were found who were quite subservient to their guidance and complied with their wishes, but nothing less would please. Many of these paintings will mark the times, and by the exagerated productions of the artists, serve to be laughed at when the folly and the self interested motives which gave birth to them are done away.

Sometime after the death of Mr Gill, he was succeeded by another hospitable friend, Thomas Maddison Esqre* of Birtley, at whose town house I spent many a social evening. He, like the former, delighted in gathering together a few friends to talk away the winter evenings, on various subjects, but never to a late hour. His most constant visitors were John Anderson, surgeon, old John Walker, patent sadler, with his friend and assistant in that business, John Hall, Captn John Reay, of the lighthouse – Low Lights, North Shields, and Charles Whitlock, comedian, and other occasional visitors. He also frequently had some of us in parties, along with him to Birtley, where he also constantly invited the Roman Catholic priest of the place and other neighbours, to partake with us of his good cheer.

* Thomas Maddison died 12 October 1811 aged 73 and was buried in Chester le Street church. He was of an independant character; he was one of the committee (the youngest) who tried the Magistrates of Newcastle respecting the Town Moor, in 1774

[155]

16

From this time 'till the peace was concluded, the same kind of political debatings continued and were almost the constant subject, in all companies; and I have often sat and listned with wonder, at the jargon of the protected fools and the impudent faces put on by those who lived upon the taxes, to hear them argue, if so it may be called, in defense of all the measures, now pursued – a great portion of these seemed to me to be smitten with blindness, and knaves and their abettors appeared to predominate or over rule the country; this they carried to such a length, that I think if Mr Pitt had proposed to make a law to transport all men who had pug noses, and to hang all men above 60 years of age, these animals (those excepted who came within the meaning of the act) would have advocated it as a brilliant thought and a wise measure. If we examine these times and look back at such like of old, we may indeed wonder at both – the inroads of ignorance have been the same. The time was (see *England's Grievance* etc by Ralph Gardner of Chirton in the year 1655) when the magistrates of Newcastle sent to Scotland for a man who was reputed as being very clever in discovering witches. He came and easily convicted many a fine woman, as well as those who were wrinkled with age and wisdom, and they were by this means tried and put to death. He returned home very rich, and as soon as General Leslie knew all the circumstances from his friends in Newcastle, he sent for this wretch to Berwick, where he then commanded his army, and hanged him at once without either judge or jury – did he do wrong?* I think, if there be a plurality of devils, ignorance must be their king. The wretchedness which ignorance has from time to time spread over the world, is truely appalling. *This is a King that should be deposed, without loss of time* – and that portion of mankind, who are under the guidance of his imps, should have nothing to do with the affairs of society and should be carefully looked to and kept out of every kind of command, and even the poor innocent unreasoning animals should, in mercy, not be allowed to be goaded and to suffer under their folly and cruelty.

To attempt giving any thing like a detail of the history of this eventfull war, would in this place be useless – that must be left to the historian. It

* This part is traditionary – Gardner says he was for such like 'villanie' hanged in Scotland – 'and upon the gallows, he confessed he had been the death of two hundred and twenty women in England and Scotland, for the gain of twenty shillings apiece, and beseached forgiveness, and was executed'.

appears to me that Mr Pitt was urged into it, chiefly by ambition and that his disappointments broke his heart. General Bonaparte, from his unparalelled victories, became in his turn blinded by ambition, which ended in his being conquered and banished to St Helena for life. He had

divided and conquered, in victory after victory, almost all his continent-al enemies, one after another, and then, mostly generously returned them their dominions back again, but this would not all do – despotism, urged on and supported by this country, was rooted too deeply in their Governments, for them to think of making any change to better the condition of their people. It would appear it is a business they cannot think of, and the old maxim with them, that the many were made only to support the few, seems continually uppermost in their resolves. If Bonaparte had been as good a man as he was a great one, he had it in his power to settle all this, and to have established the happiness of both the Governments and the people, over all the civilised world, for ages to come; but although he had the example of the incomparable Washington before him, he did not copy him. He ceased to be the first consul of France, managed to get himself made Emperour, married the princess of Austria, and became one of the Legitimates; this added to the stock of his ambition, and from that time he began to decline. Fortune at length seemed to frown upon him and the frost and snow of Russia, cut off and destroyed his immensely large and well appointed army and quickly afterwards, baffled his future strenuous efforts to repair his loss and paved the way for his defeat at Waterloo, which sealed his ruin.

One would think that the gaining of worlds, would not compensate the misery and the horrid waste of human life which are the certain attendants of war, and one would wonder, what kind of materials men are made of, or what kind of *minds and souls* direct the actions of the authors of it. Were they to reflect, it may fairly be concluded, they could not bear their own thoughts and that they would, after taking a cool survey of the wretchedness they have occasion'd, go immediately and hang themselves. But it would appear that the lives of human beings weigh little in the scale of great man-killers – they are perhaps not fitted for reflection, or perhaps only that kind of it which can look at nothing but their own misguided ambition, or private gain. It would be well for the abettors and advocates of war, to try to weigh the good and bad (setting aside the inhumanity) attendant upon such a wicked and disgracefull course of things. This we should begin at home, and instead of celebrating the birth day of the 'Heaven born Minister' – ask his admirers, how he is entitled to this, to shew the birth of *this babe of grace*, and then to compare his actions with the title his friends have thus bestowed upon him. Might not the lives of say a million of men have been saved? and better employed than cruelly wasted in this way? could he have done it? with his consumate abilities I humbly think he could. Would not these men if so directed, have been sufficient in number, to colonise or otherwise to people and civilise immense unoccupied territories, and the money wasted would have done almost any thing. Would not the men and the money have canalled Britain and Ireland from end to end, and intersected them from side to side? and also have made piers (if wanted) at the mouths of every river in the two islands and besides have converted both into gardens – but to point out more improvements would be a waste of words, with such means in hand, they might have been almost endless. Then per contra what has been done with the millions of lives and millions of money thus spent? – they have restored Legitimacy! they have restored Louis 'the desired' and Ferdinand 'the beloved'! and the Inquisition! and they are still to be called 'God's Viceregents here on earth'! – When by their actions they shew themselves deserving of such like titles, mankind will not disturb them in these their dreams; but 'till then they will continue to smile at the conceit, as well as the *glitter* they keep up to dazzel the sight only of their purblind *loving subjects*. All wars, except defensive ones, are detestable and if governments admitted morality into their institutions and were guided by its precepts, all wars would in all probability grow into disuse and cease; but hitherto that treasure of inestimable value I think has been discarded from their councils, and I cannot discover much

[158]

difference between them and the lesser banditti of old – for in the former as well as the latter they were guided by the strong disposition to rob (as soon as they thought themselves able, successfully to do so) and to shew that they thought '*might was right*'. From the feuds of the nobility down to 'Rob-in-hood, Will Scarlet and Little John', and from the ferocious combats of the Percy and Douglas on the Borders – of Johnny Armstrong and his 'eight score of Men', down to 'Adam (Yeddy) Bell', 'Clem o' the Cleugh' and 'William of Cloudsly' and the Mosstroopers, the same wicked principle guided them and their ferocious retainers to murder each other and soak the earth with their blood.

17

The game laws have for ages past been a miserable source of contention between those rendered unqualified by severe and even cruel game laws, and those who had the influence to get such laws made for their exclusive priviledge of *killing the game as their own*. To convince the intelligent poor man, that the fowls of the air were created only for the rich, is impossible and will for ever remain so. If it be pleaded that the game are fed on the lands of the latter and thus become theirs, this may indeed be carrying the notions of the sacredness of property too far, for even this ought to have its bounds; but were this conceded, as property is at present enjoyed by a rental, and as the farmers feed the game, they would appear to belong more properly to them than to any one else. In thus viewing this business, it would only appear to be an act of justice to make an express law to secure the game to the farmers as their exclusive property and putting it out of the power of the landowners of rendering such a law (by their influence) of non effect, as well as to prevent the nightly or the day-light poacher from his intrusions and his trespasses. In thus attempting to point out what may be justice and what injustice, respecting the game laws, I own I feel great repugnance in saying any thing that might have a tendancy to curtail the genteel and healthy enjoyments of the country gentleman in his field sports, which his fortune and his leisure enables him so appropriately to pursue. While, at the same time, it is greatly to be regretted that any thing – any overstretched distinctions – should ever happen to make a breach between the poor and the rich, or to make the former feel himself like an outlaw, for it ought ever to be considered that they both are members of the same community, and that equal and just laws should guide and govern men in every station of life. It is, however, a pity that the *unqualified* man cannot find his attentions engaged and his mind sufficiently excited in some other way, or by his business, than that of becoming a poacher. But the strange propensity (however unaccountable) in almost all men to kill, and the pleasureable excitement to do so, is equally strong in the gentleman sportsman, as it is in the poacher. This excitement, or an extreme desire to exhilerate the spirits and to give them energy as well as pleasure, pervades more or less the minds of all mankind and shews itself in every species of gambling, from cock fighting, dog and man fighting, hunting, horse racing and even up to the acme of excitement or excitement run mad, that of horrid war. It seems

Old Age and Heedless Youth
*The ruins are said to represent St Edmund's Roman Catholic Chapel,
Gateshead.* BM

An Angler in a River Pool BM

The Green Woodpecker NHSN

The Chaffinch BM

to be no matter what it is, that affords this kind of pleasure. I wish it could be contrived to find out something of a more rational and better sort, but be this as it may, certain it is that the heart that never tastes pleasure, shuts up, grows stiff and incapable of enjoyment, and the minds of all men ought to be unbent, at certain times. Therefore, it would appear there ought to be something or other fallen upon to whet the mind to rouse its energies in all men (especially in some constitutions) to prevent their becoming *nerveless* and hipocondriac – the worst of all diseases – in which the mind sees every thing with an obliquity of intellect, and creates numberless, cruel and imaginary evils, to continually surround and embarras itself. Only make a man who cannot employ his mind with some hobby horse or other, sit down, to know that he is provided for and has nothing to do, and it will soon be seen how ennui with benumbing steps is thrust into his mind, and what a stupid and unhappy being he is. If I have reasoned correctly in the forgoing observations, it is then desirable that sports and pastimes should be invented that might (in many cases) turn out to public good and for this purpose, I have often thought (as one of these schemes) that very small sums might be subscribed *and collected*, and to make a great amount to be given as a prize to the best shot, at a mark. The utility and national purpose of this, may at sometime or other be felt, for so long as surrounding despots can gather together immense mercinary armies they ought to be *effectually* guarded against, and they certainly might be as effectually checked by hundreds of thousands of rifle men, including in them the militia thus trained, for this kind of self defence of this kingdom at a comparatively small expense. They might have their bullets made of baked clay, and that would probably be found as efficient as those made of lead and cost almost nothing.

The last subject I shall notice, as being kept up by unjust or unequal laws, is the fisheries throughout the kingdom. The laws respecting them originated in the times of feudal tyranny – when '*might was right*' and every thing was carried with a high hand in its own way. It was easy then for an overbearing aristocracy to get grants and charters made by their influence, entirely in behalf of themselves. The rights of the community was set at nought; the rights of mankind, as members of the same community, was treated with contempt, and never entered into their deliberations. These were absorbed in feelings of self interest which was their only guide; but these days are passed away, the march of intellect is spreading over the world, and all public matters are now viewed with feelings of a very different kind, than they were when such laws were made and which ought to have become obsolete or repealed long since.

But they are still kept in force, and will continue so, as long as the potent feelings of the same overstretched self interest is made the guide of those who have the power to keep the grasp of this their antiquated hold – for such can hear no reason, against their private interest, however unanswerable it may be. No reasonable plea can ever be set up, to shew that the fish of rivers ought to be the private property of any one. Can it be pretended that because a river or a rivulet passes through an estate, whether the owner of it will or not, that the fish which breed in it, or which live in it, ought to be theirs? They are not like the game, which are all fed by the farmer, for fish cost nobody any thing, and ought only to [be] preserved so far as they may be for the public good. Therefore they, in common justice ought to belong to the public in every county through which the rivers pass, and let at a rental from the clerk of the peace and the money arising therefrom applyed to making bridges and roads, or for other county rates. Stewards ought to be appointed to receive the rents, and a committee of auditors elected annually by ballot as a check upon the management of the whole. If the fisheries were not thus rented, the public would derive little benefit from such an immense supply of food, for without they were thus disposed of, the county would soon be overrun with such numbers of poaching vagabonds, as would become intolerable. All this however ought to be considered again, for notwithstanding the selfish principle which dictated the original grants of the fisheries long since obtained, the present possessor is not to blame – and suddenly to deprive any man of what he has been accustomed to receive, may be deemed a harsh measure and in some cases a cruel one. Therefore some equitable sum ought to be paid to him at once, as a remuneration for his being entirely done with all future claims, and they ought not to be considered as an inheretance to descend to the heirs of any one. From about the year 1760 to 67 when a boy, I was frequently sent by my parents, to purchase a salmon from the fishers of the *Strike* at Eltringham Ford – at that time I never paid more, and often less than three half pence per pound (mostly a heavy guessed weight) about which they were not *nice*. Before, or perhaps about this time there had always been an article inserted in every indenture in Newcastle that the apprentice was not to be obliged to eat salmon above twice a week, and the like bargain was made, upon hiring ordinary servants. It nead not be added that the salmo tribe then teemed in abundance in the Tyne and there can be little doubt, the same immense numbers would return to it again were proper measures pursued to facilitate their passing up it from the sea, to breed. All animals excepting fish only increase, but they *multiply*, and *that* in so extraordinary a degree that, for their numbers, set all calculation at defiance. It is well known that they asscend up every river, rivulet and burn in search of proper places to deposit their spawn – and this is the case with both those kinds which quit the sea and those which never leave the fresh water. In their thus instinctively searching for proper spawning places, they make their way up to such shallows as would make one think it impossible for any animal wanting legs and feet, could ever crawl up to. Therefore every *improper* weir and dam that obstructs their free passage ought to be thrown down, as they are almost the only cause of the salmon's quitting their proper spawning places in the river to return to spawn in the sea as well as they can, where it is fair to conclude their fry or their roe are swallowed up by other fish as soon as they or it are spread abroad along the shores. It will readily be perceived that the fishers' weirs are made chiefly with a view of preventing their neighbour fishers from coming in for their due share, but were the fisheries let as before named, the different fishing places would be planned out by the stewards, as well as remedying other faults, with an impartial hand. There are besides weirs and dams, other causes which occasion the falling off of the breed of the salmon by greatly preventing them from entering and making their way up rivers, for the purpose before named – they have a great aversion to passing through impure water, and even snow water stops them, for they will lye still and wait untill it run off; likewise the filth from manufactories, as well as many tons in a year washed off the uncleaned streets of large towns *only* by heavey showers of rain – judging from those of Newcastle and Gateshead I think my estimate of the quantity may be within bounds. Were this filth in all cases led away and laid on the land it would be of great value to farmers and some persons should be appointed to do so not in a slovenly and lazy manner, but with punctuality and dispatch. In this, the health and comfort of the inhabitants ought to be considered as of great importance to them, as well as that of keeping the river as pure as possible, on account of the fish. Should the business of rectifying weirs and dams and the other evils attendant upon them and the other matters be settled, then the next necessary step to be taken should be the appointment of river conservators and vigilant guards to protect the kipper, or spawning fish, from being killed while they are in this sickly and imbecile state – for notwithstanding their being very unwholesome food, they are so easily caught that very great numbers are taken in the night and eaten by poor people who do not know how pernitious they are. But should all this be found not to answer public expectation, the time now allowed to continue the fishing, might be shortened and in

[163]

some years, if ever found necessary, the fishing might be laid in for a season. The next matter, of great importance, to be taken into consideration, is respecting what can be done to prevent the destruction of salmon (on their first entering a river and while they are in full perfection), by their most powerful and most conspicuously destructive enemy, the porpoise* – can they not, by giving premiums for catching them, be greatly thinned of their numbers? can their tough skins not be tanned, or otherwise dressed, so as to be applied to some use? can oil not be obtained from them, partly to pay for the trouble of taking these kind of fish? and lastly can they not be used as an article of food? They were eaten formerly, even by the gentry, and why not make the attempt to do so again? – perhaps by pickling or drying them, and by other aids of cookery they might be good and wholesome, for every animal in season is wholesome, and which when out of season, is quite otherwise. No doubt the old adage 'that one man's meat, is another man's poison' may be partly true – and what people have not been used to eat they seldom like or wish for – but being, at length accustomed to the taste, it is well known that food to which they once had an aversion, after a few times using it, it became very agreable. If the parent fishes of the salmo tribe were protected, the fry would soon be seen to swarm in an incredible number – and perhaps a pair of them would spawn more than all the anglers from the source to the mouth of any river could fairly catch in one season.

Having, from a boy, been an angler, it is with feelings painfully rankling in my mind, that I live in dread (from hints already given) of this kind of recreation being checked or abridged. Angling has from time immemorial been followed and ought to be indulged in unchecked by arbitrary laws, as the birthright of every one (but particularly of the sedentary and studious) for ever. It is cruel to think of debarring the fair angler by any checks whatever. The salmon fishers may, indeed, begrudge to see such fill his creel with a few scores of the fry, and say to themselves – 'he is taking away what might have returned to us full grown salmon in a short time' (for all fish, as well as birds return to the same places at which they were bred) – but for reasons, before named, their selfishness should not be attended to for a moment, and they ought

* I have seen a shoal of porpoises, off Tynemouth, swimming abreast of each other and thus occupying a space of more than a hundred yards from the shore and crossing the mouth of the river, so that no salmon coud enter it – they went backwards and forward, for more than a mile, along shore and with such surprizing rapidity, that in their course, they caused a foam to arise like the breakers of the sea, in a storm. Might not a couple of steam packets, with strong nets sweep on shore hundreds at a time?

[164]

to take the fisheries, subject to this kind of toll or imaginary greivance. I have always felt extremely disgusted at what is called proscribed waters (except fish ponds); that is, that the fish, in these waters are claimed exclusively as all their own. The disposition which sets up claims of this kind, is the same which wou'd if it could, sell the sea, and the use of the

sun and the rain. Here the angler is debarred by the surly selfish owner of the adjoining land, the pleasure of enjoying the most healthfull and comparatively the most innocent of all diversions. It unbends the minds of the sedentary and the studious, whether it may be those employed at their desks, or the 'pale artist plying his sickly trade', and enables such to return to their avocations or their studies, with renovated energy to labour for their own, or for the public good. But as any thing, however good in itself may be made a bad use of, *therefore* some regulations should be laid down as a guide to the fair anglers, in this *their legitimate right*, and some check imposed upon the poacher, who might be inclined to stop at nothing, however unfair. I think Waltonian societies would be all-suciffient to do this, if composed of men of good character and good sense. There ought to be one of these societies established in the principle town in each district and have its honorary members branched out over the more distant parts. Perhaps a fine imposed or even the frowns of the society might be sufficient to deter poachers. Their object ought to be to regulate the times for angling, and to frown out of countenance, or send to *Coventry* such as spend the whole of their time almost continually in '*beating the streams*'; they ought also to keep a watchfull eye over such as care not how, or in what manner, they take fish, so as that they may only get plenty of them. Therefore the 'Honourable Society of Waltonians' ought to use every means in their

[165]

power to protect their 'glittering inhabitants of the waters' from being unfairly taken or destroyed. *Pought* Nets ought to be prohibited; [likewise] all catching of the salmon fry, in mill races, by pulling thorn bushes into them, to stop their passing through, and then letting off the water – in this way a cart load of these have often been known to be taken at once; and another method, still more destructive than this, is far too often put in practice and that is what is called liming the burns – this ought to be utterly put a stop to by severe punishments. A clown, perhaps from ignorance, but perhaps from something worse, thinks nothing of putting a few clots of unslaked or quick lime into a pool or hole, in a burn, for the sake of killing a few trouts that he sees in it – and thus poisons the water running down to the rivulet or the river, destroying every living creature, to such a distance as might seem incredible. The attentive angler must sometimes have observed the almost invisible, insipient but living spawn in thousands appearing only like floating mud, sunning themselves on a shallow sand bank, which as soon as the water, thus poisoned, reaches them, they drop down, like mud indeed, and are no more seen. How vividly do recollections of the enjoyments angling has afforded me, return to the mind, now when those days have passed away, never more to return. Like the Patriarch of Anglers, Izzak Walton, in his pleasing volume, volumes might yet be written on the same subject to point out and depicture the beautifull scenery of woods and water sides, in the midst of which the pleasures attendant upon this exhilerating and health restoring, hungry excercise, is pursued. How many narratives of the exploits of the days thus spent, might be raked up to dwell upon when they are all over, like a pleasing dream – from mounting the last stile, which gave the first peep of the curling or the rapid stream over the little intervening dewy enambled daisey covered holme, boundered by the early sloe and the hawthorn blossomed hedge – and in succession hung with festoons of the wild rose, the tangling woodbine and the bramble, with their bewitching foliage and the fairey ground; and the enchantment of the music of the lark, the blackbird, the throstle and the blackcap and rendered soothing and plaintive by the cooings of the ringdove which altogether charmed, but *perhaps retarded* the march to the brink of the scene of action, with its willows, its alders, or its saughs, where early commenced the day's patient *campaigne*.

The pleasing excitements of the angler still follow him, whether he is engaged in his pursuits amidst scenery like such as I have attempted to describe – or on the heathery moor, by burns guttered out by mountain torrents and boundered by rocks or grey moss covered stones, which

[166]

form the rapids and the pools in which is concealed his beautifull yellow and spotted prey. Here when tired and alone, I used to open my wallet, or pocket, and *dine on* fat meat and coarse rye bread, with an appetite that made me smile at the trouble people put themselves to in prepareing the sumptuous feast. The only music in attendance, was perhaps the murmuring burn, the whistling cry of the curlew, the solitary water ouzel or the whirring wing of the moor game. I woud however recommend to anglers not to go thus alone – a trio of them is better, and mutual assistance is often necessary. It is foreign to my purpose to give any history, in this place, of the various kinds of fishes which anglers pursue; and of this there is no nead, for I think more treatises on this subject than on any other (except sermons) have been printed to direct the angler to perfection in his art. But I cannot help noticing it as a pity that more pains have not been taken to *multiply* fish, and to increase the breed of eels, than has been done, as every permanent pool might so easily be fully stocked with them – and they are, when properly cooked the most delicious of all fish kind. Walton has been particular in describing his mode of cooking them – but unless he killed them before hand – his method is a very cruel one, and is, besides of not much consequence. After being killed they then only nead to be gutted and cooked unskinned, in an unabating heat, 'till they are done enough, for if they are cooked on a slow fire, they are apt to turn oiley and often disagree with some stomachs.

In thus dwelling on subjects which stimulate man eagerly to pursue the work of destruction and to extend his power over these animals of which he considers himself as the lord and master, and that they are destined to contribute to his pleasures or to his support, yet he ought not totally [to] forget that what is sport to him is death to them* – and the less of cruelty that can be avoided the better.

I think had I not begun so early to be an angler, and before feelings of tenderness had ever entered the mind, my eagerness for angling might have been on this score somewhat abated; but I argued myself into a belief that fish had little sense and scarcely any feeling – and they certainly have very much less of either, than any of the land animals. But we see, through all nature, that one kind of animals seem destined to live upon others – and fishes are the most voracious of all.

Before concluding this memoir, it would be ungratefull in me, not to acknowledge my obligations to my well-wishers, who have through life been steady in their friendships, and also in conferring their favors in

* One of our humane poets says 'Take not away the life you cannot give, all creatures have an equal right to live.'

the way of business – but a long list of names might seem tedious – and many of them are long ago numbered with the dead. For several years I had the favors of all the banks in Newcastle, as well as those of most of the fitters, but a steady underhand dark influence detatched several of both of these different employments from me. The first of friends to whom my thanks are due, is the Corporation of Newcastle for their long and unabating favors, as a body, and from time to time all its members individually – the most particular one of these was Alderman Archibald Reed Esqre. Among many of such friends, as I had reason to respect, both privately and publickly, one of the oldest in intimacy, affability and kindness was Anthony Easterby Esqre now of Coxlodge. Another whose eye of kindness watched my struggles to prosperity, was Mr Edmund Robson, patent sadler and hardwareman, who upon his suspecting, that in my publications, I might be labouring under difficulties, he called me out of Swarley's club room, to say that he had two hundred pounds at my service whenever I pleased; this I considered as an uncommon thing in the world, but I startled at the idea of getting into any kind of debt – so I thanked him sincerely and declined his kind offer. Two other friends of whom I had a high opinion for their truth and integrity were William Leadbitter, sadler and hardwareman, and Francis Coates, bookseller – the former died 3d August 1801 aged 38, and the latter on the 24 February 1803. An intimacy of long standing had subsisted between the Crawhall family and mine and I had a particular regard for two of the brothers – Thomas and Joseph; the latter was particularly an amateur of the arts and excelled as a painter, for which nature had furnished him with the requisite innate powers – but in this he was taken off by his business of a rope maker. I might name others of the like character but they also have departed this world long ago. A few of such only being left, both as friends and social companions – thus noticing them puts me in mind of its being like creeping out of the world as at least out of this kind of society – for excepting that of my own happy fire side – I think I shall bid all adieu. My warm friend Mr William Maving, brush manufacturer, his brother Robert, builder, Mr Alexander Reed, china dealer, Mr Adam Hutton, hardwareman, Mr William Wilson, solicitor, Mr Robert Gruisburn, stationer (and occasionally some others) were the last with whom I spent my social evenings. *The full Moon* was generally the signal for our assembling, when we gave full vent to whatever was uppermost in our minds – this was called 'getting the froth off our stomachs'.

At other times, some of my evenings were spent much in the same way in company with John Marshall, printer, and others, along with

John Ambrose Williams, the Editor of the *Durham Chronicle* – in which paper, he had spoken freely of the Durham clergy, respecting their conduct towards the Queen – little suspecting that they had 'till this day, kept ready by them as much of the sour liven of old as was sufficient to puff up or foment the lump of their clerical pride and dignity to an overflowing height. In short, with their prosecutions and persecutions and law suits, they ruined this clever *advocate for liberty and patriotic man*. It might be tedious to swell out a list of names or dwell upon the occasional visits of men of sense and ability who from time to time spent their evenings with me. Mr Anthony Scott of Southwick pottery was one of these, and when he was in Newcastle he seldom missed this kind of social exchange of our sentiments. On these occasions my ingenious self taught friend Mr Robert Wilson, engineer and engine maker always made one of our party. In their company the longest evening seemed very short. I was also often visited by *poor old* Mr John Rastrick of Morpeth who, in his day, was by many men of judgment accounted one of the most able and ingenious engineers in the kingdom – he died [in] June 1826 Æt 88. I also spent much time (while he remained in Newcastle) with my gallant friend Col. Wemys, of Wemys Hall in Fife Shire, formerly of the 11th Regt of Foot and afterwards Col. of the Fife Shire Militia – he was ardent in his pursuit after mechanical knowledge and greatly valued ingenious work men in that way – and begged I would introduce him to such. He said 'he cared not what kind of coat they wore' and I was not long in introducing him to such, in whose company he gained the desired information he wanted, and seemed highly gratified.

[169]

18

Not having seen Edinburgh since August 1776, I longed to see it again, and accompanied with my Jane and Isabella, we set off on this journey on the 11th of August 1823 and went through, by coach, on that day. I always thought highly of Edinburgh and its bold and commanding situation – but the new town (or city of palaces, as it is now sometimes called) had been added to it since that time; but all these splendid buildings, are of trivial import, compared with the mass of intellect and science, which had taken root and been nurtured and grown up to such a height as to rival and perhaps outstrip every other city in the world. Our stay in it was only a fortnight and this was a busy time with us, both as to its being taken up with the kindness and hospitality we met with every where, as well as in visiting its various scientific and other establishments. It being at a vacation season, when most of the learned professors were out of town, we saw only Professors Jameson and Wallace, and the kindness of these gentlemen I never can forget. We were often at the table of the former, surrounded by men of learning and science who visited him, on which occasions, the amiable manners and affability of his sisters, the Misses Jameson, made every place appear like a home. The civility of Professor Wallace was also of the most friendly complexion. He shewed me the use of the Eidograph, an instrument which he invented for the purpose of either reducing or enlarging any drawing or design, accurately, to any size that might be wished for. We also visited Mr Patrick Neil, along with the Misses Jameson, and were besides greatly pleased with seeing his tamed birds and other curiosities which embellished his little paradise – his uncommon kindness will ever remain impressed upon our memories. We also often called upon my friend Mr Archibald Constable – accounted the first bookseller in Scotland, ('tho ill at the time) and partook of his kind attentions. Mr Robert Miller, bookseller, also did every thing in his power which affability and kindness could dictate to make us altogether pleased with Edinburgh. Our friend Mr William Reid, bookseller, Leith did the same, only with this difference, that his attentions were unceasing, and Mrs Reid and his hospitality made their house a kind of home to us; almost constantly accompanied by Mr Reid, as our guide, we visited *every place*, and he besides introduced me to such artists as I did not know. In this way he took us to Mr William Allen, the historical painter – to the rooms of the splendid exhibition of the paintings of the

[170]

late Sir Henry Raeburn Bart – to Mr [James] Stewart, the engraver – to
Mr Howe, the portrait and animal painter and to the painting rooms of
others who were absent. To some other artists who were known to me, I
spent some time in several calls – these consisted of my old friend, Mr
[Alexander] Nasmyth, the excellent landskip painter, my townsmen Mr
William Nicholson and Mr [John] Ewbank both of whom were eminent
painters, and Mr Thomas Coulson distinguished in his line as an
ornamental and house painter. I also made some calls upon Mr James
Kirkwood, now up in years and past his work, but who had in his prime
led the way to excellence, particularly in writing engraving, in which he
was succeeded by his son and grandson. I also paid my respects to the
son and successor of my kind friend of former days, the late Mr Hector
Gavin, and the same to the sons and successors of the late Mr D. Lizars,
all these in my estimation were doing credit to their instructors as
engravers – and all these artists, as well as the painters, had attained
in their various ways to that degree of excellence which did honour to
Edinburgh, now the seat of learning, and rendered brilliant by the gems
both of arts and sciences with which it is adorned. We left Edinburgh on
the 23d of August 1823 and I think I shall see Scotland no more. I think
so well of these, our northern countrymen, both English and Celtic, that
in most things they may serve as a pattern of both good sense and good
conduct worthy of imitation by the other less civilized nations of the
world. I have almost forgot to name my being introduced to Messrs
Ballantyne and Robertson, the lithographic printers – while I was in
their office, the latter pressed me to make a sketch on the stone for him.
We were then preparing to leave Edinburgh, and the only time left me
was so short that I was obliged to do this sketch before breakfast the
next morning, and they got proofs from it the same day. In doing this,
'tho very slight, I could see what that manner of making prints was
capable of performing.

After my journeys (long ago) to Cherry-burn were ended, I used as formerly, seldom to miss going in the mornings to Elswick Lane to drink whey or butter milk. In this I commonly fell in with a party who went there for the same purpose, and this kind of social intercourse continued for many years.

I also, at that time, on the Sunday afternoon, frequently went to visit and contemplate in the church yards and there give vent to my mind in feelings of regret, and in repeating to myself a kind of soliloquy over the graves of those with whom I had been

> *And then, I loved to haunt lone burial places*
> *Pacing the Church-yard earth with noisless tread*
> *To pore in new-made graves for gastly traces*
> *Brown crumbling bones of the forgotten dead.*

intimate – but as this at length appeared to be unavailing sorrow, I left it off – recounting in my memory the numbers of my friends thus put by, to be forgotten among the millions of others, who had been, at longer and shorter periods also, in this world passed away into oblivion. Some men from the first, as soon as they die, are quite unnoticed, some are remembered only for a day and some a little while longer, and even the 'frail memorials', erected to *perpetuate the memory* of those who had been esteemed by some, seemed to me to be of as little avail, and their mementos as well as those decked out with ornamented flatteries, in time would all go to decay and be remembered no longer than untill all who once knew them were also dead. And the numbers of both the one and the other appeared to me so immense, that to estimate them seemed impossible and like attempting to count the grains of sand on the sea beach, which had been tossed to and fro and then left by the waves. It is thus that the grave swallows all up without distinction – the true esti-mate of their various characters and merits can only be known to the creator of all, who, according to the reasoning and instinctive powers given by him, in a greater or lesser degree, to all mankind – but called forth only by those whose souls habitually adore and commune with God, while they remain in this stage of probation – to these it appears clear that he will, in his infinite goodness, wisdom, truth, justice and mercy, on quitting this mortal abode, place every one in the unknowable worlds appointed for and befitting their reception – but notwithstanding the temporary mementos, dedicated to private worth, thus described – to others of a different or public character they may have their use; and as no man ever lived that was not better pleased with being praised than blamed, the minds of such may be soothed by the good opinion of their fellow men. Therefore monuments [might be] erected to those who have by their virtues and patriotism promoted the happiness of mankind – [they] ought to have every respect paid to their memories. It is a debt of gratitude, due from the public to the author of our being for the loan of departed worth, and may stimulate others to 'do so likewise' 'tho the posthumous praise or blame of the world, is to them of no avail – they are done with all things on this side of time and are out of the reach of both the one and the other. While I was pursuing my wild (Goose chase) ramblings in the Highlands and beheld with admiration the great projecting rocks, so often to be seen holding up their bare useless heads to the winds, it struck me that it was a great pity they could not be converted to a better use, and that as the best I could think of was that the names of their illustrious worthies Wallace and Bruce, as well as their other worthies, should be inscribed upon them – to hold up their heads with these names to the sun *for ever*. I have often since that time thought that the bare rocks in other parts of our islands might with good effect be filled up in the same way. And the first name to be fixed upon ought to be Alfred the Great, followed by many others – statesmen – patriots – philosophers – poets etc – who have shone out like polished diamonds and who have embellished and illumined this country and civilized the world. Their venerated names with their maxims, or quotations from their works, would fill up many of these rocks (which are waiting for them) and might make all who beheld them be inclined to profit by or to imitate their virtues. How many incomparably good, wise, and *beautifull* texts from the Bible, might also with great propriety be added to fill up every vacant spot. I often lamented that I had not the means to enable me to be at the expense of getting inscriptions and such like quotations inscribed in this way. Often, while I was angling by the watersides, in a hot sunny day, which slackened my sport, I have sat down and thought over some of the beautifull lines of our poets fit to be

[173]

applied in this way – and remember well my having first thought of those from Cunningham's poems – which I would, if I could have afforded it, have *committed to the care of a rock* – he says

> *How smooth that silent River glides*
>   *Progressive to the deep*
> *the poppies pendant o'er its sides*
>   *have soothed the waves to sleep.*
> *Pleasure's intoxicated Sons!*
> *Ye indolent! ye gay! reflect!*
> *for as the river runs, time wings*
>   *his trackless way*

This is from memory

    How easy would it be for gentlemen to get the names of the illustrious dead thus inscribed upon rocks; or where that could not be done, to erect pillars or small obelisks over copious springs (like the holy wells of old) to contain such inscriptions as those I have hinted at and thus leave this their marks behind them; and which would long continue to put the passing stranger in mind of some religious, moral or patriotic sentiment, and while he was refreshing himself by quenching his thirst, he might be put in mind that

> *Man wants but little here below*
> *Nor wants that little long*

19

Having already noticed my beginnings, or first efforts, in engraving on wood, and as at that time this branch of the arts, was at the very lowest ebb in this country, and I believe also, in every other country in Europe – it may perhaps be of some use, or at least may excite some curiosity to know the part I took in renewing or bringing into use (this to me) new art, as far as I was able with the slender means in my hands, and the many difficulties [I had] to contend with and surmount, before any thing like an approach towards perfection could be arrived at. I ought first distinctly to state, that it never entered into my head that it was a branch of art that would stand preeminent for utility, or that it could ever in the least compete with engraving on copper. I ought also to observe, that no vain notions of my ever arriving at any eminence ever passed thro' my mind, and that the sole stimulant with me was the pleasure I derived from imitating natural objects (and I had no other patterns to go by) and the opportunity it afforded me of making and drawing my designs on the wood, as the only way I had in my power of giving vent to a strong propensity to gratify my feelings in this way. In process of time however, as I began to improve, and then seeing the practical use printers were making of wood cuts, the utility and importance of them began to be unfolded to my view; and the more I have since thought upon the subject, the more I am confirmed in the opinions I have entertained, that the use of wood cuts would know no end – or so long as the great importance of printing was duly appreciated and the liberty of the press held sacred. The first difficulty, I felt, as I proceeded, was in getting the cuts I had done, printed so as to look any thing like my drawings on the blocks of wood, or in corresponding to the labour I had bestowed upon the cutting of the designs. At that time pressmen were utterly ignorant as to any proper effect that was to be produced – or even if one of them possessed any notions of excellence bejond the common run of workmen, his materials for working were so defective that he could not execute even what he himself wished to accomplish. The common pelt balls then in use, so daubed the cut and blurred and overlapped its edges, that the impression looked disgusting. To remedy this defect, I was obliged carefully to shave down the edges round about, and this answered the end I had in view. The next difficulty was worse to surmount, and required a long time to get over it, and that was to lower down the surface on all the parts I wished to

[175]

appear pale, so as to give the appearance of the required distance – and this process will always continue to call forth and to exercise the judgement of every wood engraver, even after he knows what effect his *carefull pressman* may be enabled to produce, from his manner of cutting. On this all artists must form their own ideas. I think no exact description can be laid down by him as a rule for others to go by – they will, by practice, have to find out this themselves. While I was patiently labouring and contending with difficulties, which I could not over come, I was shown some impressions from wood cuts done long ago, with cross hatching such as I thought I should never be able to execute – these were wood cuts by Albert Durer and perhaps some others of his day, in the collection of the Revd John Brand (the Newcastle historian) and from these I concluded that Albert Durer must have had some very easy way of loading his blocks with such an useless profusion of cross hatching, or he would not have done them so, without he had found out some easy means of etching the wood (or perhaps metal plates), quite unknown to me; but if otherwise, I then, in changing my opinion, could think of no other way than that he must have cut his blocks on the plank side of the wood, on which it would be more easy to pick out the interstices between the squares or the lozened shaped lines, than as I (at that time) thought it possible to do on the end way of the wood. One of these plank blocks, said to have been drawn by Albert Durer, was shewn to me by my kind friend George Allan Esqr of the Grange, Darlington – the drawing, which was done with great accuracy, seemed to me to have been done by a crow quill with a kind of varnish ink, the strokes of which from their regularity looked as if they had been printed from a well executed copper plate, and transferred to the block. After labouring for some time in endeavouring to produce the like effect on my blocks, on the end way of the wood, not indeed to my satisfaction, I felt mortified in not succeeding to my wish and I then begun to think the impressions must have been printed from two blocks. This indeed I soon found to be quite easy to do, as well as being beautifully correct, and any artist may see this in a few minutes, by cutting parallel lines on a piece of wood, and from it, taking by his hand, an impression on a piece of paper, and then again inking the same cut, and printing it in the same way, either directly in a cross, or in an oblique direction upon the first impression – this can also be easily done, from two cuts, at a printing press, and is much easier to do and better than the labour necessarily bestowed upon one cross hatched block. When I had accomplished this, and satisfied myself that the process was both simple and perfect, as to obtaining the object I so much wanted, my curiosity on this score

[176]

The Snowman at Cherryburn

Bewick's birthplace appears in the background; the figure on the stool is said to be a self-portrait. BM

The Robin BM

An Early Morning Thief Surprised NHSN

The Boy and the Nest
'We must bow to fate in trusting to a rotten stick.'

ceased, and I then begun to conclude that in this way the cross hatching might be set aside as a thing of no use at all. The artists, indeed, of the present day have brought it to such a pitch of perfection, that I do not know that it can be carried any further; and in this they have also been so marvellously aided by the improved methods now used in printing their cuts, that one would be led to conclude this department has also attained to perfection, and had not this been the case, the masterly execution of wood cuts either by crossed lines, or otherwise, would have continued to be beheld with disgust or contempt. I have long been of opinion that the cross hatching of wood cuts, for book work, was a waste of time, as every desired effect can be much easier obtained by plain parallel lines, and that the other way was not the legitimate object of wood engraving; and that instead of their drawing and imitating the manner of copper etchings, with great labour and time on the wood, such drawings might have been as soon etched on the copper at once; and where a large impression of any publication was not wanted, the copper plate would have cost less, and lasted long enough for the purpose intended. I never could discover any additional beauty or colour that the crossed strokes gave to the impression, bejond the effect produced by plain paralel lines, and this is very apparent when to a certainty the plain surface of the wood, will print as black as ink and balls can make it, without any further labour at all; and it may easily be seen that the thinest strokes cut upon the plain surface, will throw *some light* on the subject or design, and if these strokes are made wider and deeper, it will reccive more light, and if these strokes again are made still wider, or of equal thickness to the black lines, the colour these produce will be a grey – and the more the white strokes are thick'ned, the nearer will they in their varied shadings approach to white – and if quite taken away, then a perfect white is obtained. The methods I have pursued, appear to me to be the simple and easy perfection of wood engraving, for book printing – and, no doubt will appear, better and worse according to the abilities of the artists who execute them. The first time I ever heard any thing about colour being produced by plain engraving, was in the compliments bestow'd upon me by Dr Thomas Stout for my engraving on a large silver box for him. The device or design, I have now forgot, but never what he said upon the occasion, and from that time I attempted *colour* upon the wood, and though I felt much difficulty in my attempts at producing it, yet the principle is there and will shine out under the skill and management of any eminent engraver on wood who is gifted with a painter's eye, and his work will be complete if seconded by a pressman of ability, who may happen to have

[177]

a talent and fellow feeling for the art. I have before noticed my lowering down the surface of the wood in order to produce the effect of distance, and the same thing holds good with every figure, where different shades of colour is desired – leaving the surface of the block without being pared down at all, and relying only on the lines being left thicker or smaller for producing the requisite depth of shade, this surface thus left, acts as a support to the more delicate lines which have been engraved upon the lowered part of the cut. After all the parts are thus lowered, a further paring down of the edges of the various figures which the cut contains, may be necessary to prevent their appearing as if surrounded by a white line. The delicate lines thus lowered so as [to] print pale or distant parts, and thus protected by the stronger lines left on the surface, a wood cut (with care) will print an incredible number – how many, it may be difficult exactly to say, but it once happened that I had the opportunity given me of guessing pretty nearly at this, and it was from the calculations of the late Mr Solomon Hodgson, who once called upon me along with a gentleman (a stranger to me) who seemed extremely curious to know every thing about engraving on wood – and one of his queries was with a view to enable him exactly to know how many impressions a wood cut could print, before it was worn out. Not having any thing in mind at the moment to enable me to satisfy him, I begun to consider and then it struck me that a little delicate cut, a view of Newcastle, was done for Mr Hodgson many years before as a fac for his newspaper. I then got out my ledger to shew him the date when it was done – he at first startled and said 'it must have printed a million!' He however sat down and calculated exactly, and found it had printed above 900,000. This cut was continued in the paper several years afterwards, untill the columns of it were altered. This cut was protected in the manner before noticed, by a strong black line, or border, surrounding it, within which the surface was lowered, previous to cutting the view. This cut is still kept, and except being somewhat damaged by being tossed about in a drawer among other cast away cuts, it might (by being a little repaired) yet print many thousands. This is mentioned with a view to show the great length of time that cuts, done in this way, will last, if they are carefully adjusted to the height of the type, and kept out of the hands of ignorant rude pressmen. I am of opinion that cuts done in the manner called 'surface cutting' cannot stand any thing like so large an impression, as when they thus are lowered, for the delicate lines, when left on the surface must soon break down, from the heavy pressure to which they are exposed.

[178]

20

It is foreign to my present purpose to criticise the works of brother artists of the present day. I behold their excellent productions with pleasure; in them there is no falling off: they surpass those of the artists of the *olden times*.

I cannot, however, help lamenting that in all the vicissitudes which this art has undergone, some species of it is lost and done away – I mean the large blocks, with the prints from them, so common to be seen when I was a boy, in every cottage and farm house throughout the whole country. These blocks, I suppose must, from their size, have been cut the plank way on beech or some other kind of close grained wood, and from the immense number of impressions from them, so cheaply and extensively spread over the whole country, must have given employment to a great number of artists in this inferiour department of wood cutting, and must also have formed to them an important article of traffick. These prints, which were sold at a very low price, were commonly illustrative of some memorable exploits – or perhaps the portraits of emminent men who had distinguished themselves in the service of their country, or in their patriotic exertions to serve mankind; besides these, there were a great variety of other designs, often with songs added to them, of a moral, a patriotic or a rural tendancy which served to enliven the circle in which they were admired. To enumerate the great variety of these *pictures* would be a task. A constant one in every house, was 'King Charles's Twelve Good Rules'; representations of remarkable victories at sea, and battles on land, [were] often accompanied with portraits of those who commanded and others who had born a conspicuous part in those contests with the enemy. The house in Ovingham, where our dinner poke was taken care of, when at school, was hung round with views or representations of the battles of Zondorf and several others – the portraits of Tom Brown the valiant Granadier – Admiral Haddock – Admiral Benbow and other portraits of admirals – a figure or representation of the Victory man-of-war of 100 guns, commanded by Admiral Sir John Balchen, and fully manned with 1100 picked seamen and volunteers, all of whom and this uncommonly fine ship were lost – *sunk to the bottom of the sea* – this was accompanied with a poetical lament of the catastrophe, part of which was 'ah hapless Victory, what avails thy towering masts, thy spreading sails'. Some of the portraits I recollect were now and then to be met with, which were

[179]

very well done in this way, on wood. In Mr Gregson's kitchen one of this character hung against the wall many years – it was a remarkably good likeness of Captn Coram. In cottages every where were to be seen the sailor's farewell and his happy return – youthfull sports, and the feats of Manhood – the bold Archers shooting at a mark – the four Seasons etc. Some subjects were of a funny and others of a grave character. I think the last portraits I remember of, were those of some of the rebel lords and 'Duke Willy'. These kind of wood cut pictures are long since quite gone-out of fashion, which I feel very sorry for and most heartily wish they could be revived again. It is desirable indeed, that the subjects should be well chosen, for it must be of great importance that such should be the case – as whatever can serve to instill morality and patriotism into the minds of the whole people, must tend greatly to promote their own happiness, and the good of the community; for all men, however poor they may be, ought to feel that *this* is their country, as well as it is that of the first noblemen in the land, and if so, they will be equally as interested in its happiness and prosperity. There is another way, not yet indeed entered upon, of similar import as the foregoing, in which prints might with good effect be made of subjects fit to embellish almost every house throughout our country, and that is from wood blocks, printed in colours, like paper hangings. Having seen some such done by paper stainers, so as almost to equal good paintings – this leads me to wish that this method could be pursued for the same ends as those already noticed. The most remark-able productions of art of this kind, from blocks done to print in colours, like beautifull little paintings, were sent to me by Mr Gubitz of Berlin; they might indeed be said to be perfection. Several impressions from duplicate, or triplicate blocks, done and printed in this way, of a very large size, were also given to me, as well as a drawing of the press from which they were printed many years ago, by an old man of the name of Jackson ('Jean Baptiste Jackson') who had been patronized by the King of France; but whether these prints had been done with the design of embellishing the walls of houses in that country I know not – they had been taken from paintings of the eminent old Masters and were mostly scripture pieces. They were well drawn and perhaps correctly copied from the originals, yet in my opinion none of them looked well. Jackson left Newcastle quite enfeebled with age, and it was said, ended his days in an asylum, under the charitable and protecting care of Sir Gilbert Elliot Bart, at some place on the border near the Teviot or on Tweed-side. Whether the speculations, here noticed, may be thought worthy of being acted upon, or otherwise I know not. But it is not in any of the above noticed ways of woodcutting that my attention is directed; it is in my ardent desire to see the *stroke* engraving on wood carried to the utmost perfection, and done in the way now pursued, that I hope the *world* will be gratified; and I trust the time is not distant when its superiour excellence will be seen, particularly in landscape scenery, so as to surpass copper engravings. The effect to be produced by wood engraving has not (in that way) yet been tried and its powers are not made apparent – and this is, I think, to be attained by two, or even more blocks being used, on one print, that a greater and more natural effect, as to colour and softness is to be produced. I am well aware that some difficulty may arise, as to bringing off a clear impression of fine strokes from so large a surface, but in this age of mechanical improvement and invention, I think this apparent difficulty will readily be got over – perhaps printing from a roller, instead of an even down pull, might easily accomplish this business. I have often thought, had William Woolett been a wood engraver, he would have shewn its excellence long ago; his prints from copper have not been equalled, but from the nature of the wood and the effect it produces, he would have advanced a step farther and on it have outdone his excellence on copper. If I live (health and sight continued) I will make the attempt to shew that all this is not a visionary theory. Should I not live to get this memoir printed under my own inspection, for the *benefit* of yourself, your brother and sisters – or whether it will ever be printed at all, I know not, but at any rate the manuscript itself, which I leave to my dear Jane, will satisfy her (were that necessary) how ardently I have ever wished well to arts and artists, and 'tho in my endeavours to shew this, I have often been thwarted and disappointed – yet I never lost sight of my object nor became dis-heartened, in my struggles to fight through and surmount numberless difficulties and barrs thrown in my way. You know a part of those I met with in the course of my business, in which my time was misspent, and also the waste of it bestow'd upon useless and wicked pupils. I know you wish me to give you a history and description of such, but to do so would be an irksome task and I cannot now be troubled to think about it. I shall however give you a curtailed list (as a whole) and only speak of such as served out their time. I have already noticed my brother John as my first pupil, and therefore have little further to say respecting him – but only further by adding that nature seemed to have befitted him for becoming a first rate wood engraver; but at the time he was with me, the thoughts of aiming at excellence did not enter into our heads, and he left this world at the time when it was only begun to be looked upon as a matter of any interest. Our first apprentice was John Laws, who was

[181]

brought up as a silver engraver and I think he never touched upon the wood; his turn was directed to the ornamental and chiefly in the branch of what is called bright engraving and at this kind of work he excelled, and is perhaps the best at this day; with it he also follows the business of a farmer at 'Heddon Laws', the place of his nativity. We greatly respected him for his honesty, sobriety, civil deportment and attention. The next for whom we had a great regard, for the like reasons, was John Johnson, and who we put to do engraving on wood, as well as other kinds of work; I think he would have shone out in the former branch, but he died of a fever, at about the age of 22 when only beginning to give great promise of his future excellence. Our next apprentice was Robert Johnson who did not incline to do wood cutting, and prefering copper plate engraving he was almost wholly employed in that way and in it attained to great excellence; and besides that, he became great as a draftsman and colourist. But as he was of so delicate a constitution that he could not bear confinement, we for that reason set him to work to make sketches and views, where he had both air and exercise. It may be necessary to give a more detailed history, than ordinary, of this boy, on account of the unceasing pains I bestowed upon his tuition and my reasons for doing so. His mother had been long a servant in father's house, where she became a great favourite and like one of our own family. When she married, this boy Robert was her first born; and when he was christned I was to have been his godfather. This however did not happen, for while I was, for that purpose, on my road near to Ovingham, where the ceremony was to be performed, being only about 16 or 17 years old and exceedingly bashfull, I could not think of appearing before a congregation of people; and when, on getting to the top of the 'Pantin Brae' the bells began to ring in for Church, I felt so abashed at the thoughts of what I had to do that I 'turned tails', went a little back, and crossed the river upon the top of the Fishermen's Weir by stepping from one stob to another, which are driven in to support the wicker work and stones of which the weir is formed. I then went to Cherryburn and after getting some refreshment, returned again to Newcastle. In the mean time my father and mother stood sponsors for the child. As the boy grew up, he having been almost constantly told he was to be my apprentice, he looked up to me as a kind of deity, and having been, at every opportunity, kept closely employed in drawing, and *'making pictures'*, which were regularly shewn to my father and mother, and through them to my self, he thus came very early into practice. As soon as he attained somewhere about his 13th year, his friends began to act upon the plan so long intended of putting these intentions in force, and

[182]

in this business my father and mother stood formost, as the warm friends of the boy, and begged I would always shew the same disposition towards him and to take him under my fostering care. He was about a year too young to be bound as an apprentice, but I took him into my house 'till the proper time arrived, when he was bound to my partner and myself for seven years. He was mostly employed in drawing, and was also at intervals practising himself in the use of the graver and in etching on copper, but being very delicate in his health, we were carefull not to confine him too closely at any thing. It may perhaps be usefull to artists to know how I thought it best to order and manage such a tender and pampered boy. The system I begun upon was that of a

rigid temperance – he got no medicine from me. My sister Ann, at that time kept my house, and to get her to second me in my plans, I experienced great difficulty, chiefly from her fears 'that folks would raise a report that we hungered him', but I resolutely persisted in my plan and would not allow her to put in her word against it. I began by cutting off, for him, almost every thing he had given him to eat. The animal food with which I helped his plate at dinner, did not exceed in bulk the size of three of my fingers; to this was added, a portion of vegetables. For breakfast and supper he got a pint of milk, with leavened rye bread, to which last article I did not prevent him from helping himself. He had not been kept to this kind of temperate or pinched regimen about two months, 'till such an alteration for the better took place in his looks as seemed surprizing, so much so that his mother, when she called to see him, held up her hands in astonishment at seeing this change from a pale, pasty, sickly look, to that of his having cheeks blushed with health like a rose and this same method was pursued while he remained under my roof.* The methods I took to learn him his

* Another of my plans was to make growing boys exercise with dumb bells half an hour or so before bed time. I believe were this practised by the sedentary of both sexes – it would go a great way to banish consumption.

[183]

business was also of a piece with his mode of living. I did not keep him so long at work, as to tire him, with whatever job he might be put to do, but especially in drawing; but then, whatever I gave him to copy, was to be done *perfectly correct*, and he dreaded to shew me work that was not so, altho' I never scolded him, but only, if I was not pleased, I put the drawing away from me without saying a word – sometimes indeed I remember of saying 'O fie!' and in this way of treatment he attained to great accuracy. The next thing I put him to was that of colouring, chiefly my own designs, and these occasioned me much time and labour, for I made it a point of drawing these with great accuracy, and with a very delicately pencilled outline. The practical knowledge I had attained in colouring was imparted to him and he saved me a great deal, of what I considered a loss of my time in being taken up in this way; and besides he soon coloured them in a stile superiour to my hasty pro-ductions of that kind – indeed, in this way he became super-excellent, and as I conceived he could hardly be equalled in his water coloured drawings of views and landscapes, by any artist. For some time, I continued to sketch in his figures, but at length he neaded none of my help in this way. I remember of his once coming to me and begging I would draw or sketch in a tree for him. 'No Robert,' said I, 'but I will direct you to a place, where you will see such a tree as you never saw painted by any artist, in your life', and that was a tree then growing in *Adonis's Grove*. He went and endeavoured to do justice to his pattern, and I do not know that any one could have made a better likeness. As soon as the time arrived that he became entitled to have wages from us, this tempted his father and mother to leave the country and to reside in Newcastle and to have him to board with them. How he was managed as to his diet with them I know not, but it soon appeared to have been a wrong treatment in this respect, for he soon lost his health and was from that time seldom out of the hands of the doctor; and at one period of his apprenticeship he was about a year absent from our employment, either in the country or in being nursed with watchfull care at home. He however became quite well by the time he was freed from his servitude with us, and he then commenced painting and engraving on his own account. In the former art he seemed to be much patronized, and had, I believe, turned his attention to oil painting. The last of his efforts in this line, was done under the patronage of the Earl of Breadalbane, by whom he was employed to copy some portraits and perhaps some other things at [Kenmore] where he took ill of a fever and died in the year 1796 and in the 26th of his age – and was buried there. It always appeared to me, that he would have become great as a painter, but a delicate constitution and want of stamina prevented this. I have often thought it was a great mistake in parents and a very common one, to fix upon some sedentary employment for their *tender delicate boy*, when perhaps, had he been sent to sea, or some other out door work, where he would be exposed to fresh air and exercise, he might have become a healthy stout man. My friends having often expressed a wish, that I would give some account of my pupils, has occasioned me to dwell thus long on that of Robert Johnson – but I think it unnecessary to notice others, who were not gifted with talents, and some others again who had neither one good property nor another and with whom I had much vexation and much reason to complain. The first of my pupils who after my brother, made a figure in London as a wood engraver, was Charlton Nesbit. He went at a nick of time, when wood cuts seemed to claim something like universal attention, and fortunately for that art it was under the guidance of the ingenious John Thurston* who pencilled his designs stroke by stroke on the wood with the utmost accuracy, and it would appear that Nesbit was the first, by his mechanical excellence, to do justice to these designs. Henry Hole† and John Anderson preceded Nesbit.

The next of my pupils who chiefly turned his attention to wood engraving was Edward Willis, who while he remained with me was much upon a par with Nesbit, but did not equal him in the mechanical excellence Nesbit had attained to in London. I had a great regard for Edward Willis on account of his regular good behaviour while he was under my tuition; he has now been long a resident in London. My

* John Thurston was reared from a child at a place called the Leases, near Newcastle, where a burn separates a large pasture, (which goes by that name) from the 'Town Moor'. His Mother, who lived at Scarbro, where the boy was born, had married a second husband, who it appears was of a base character, and had married her solely for her property – this her friends saw and to prevent her ruin, sent her off incog: to the forenamed place, to be out of the way of the worthless fellow; and my friend, John Anderson, Surgeon, was deputed to advance her the money, necessary for her support. The boy was afterwards sent to the Academy of the ingenious Mr Hornsey at Scarbro', to finish his education and with him he also learned to draw. Mr Hornsey made the designs for the *Copper Plate Magazine* and for other things and was author of 'Hornsey's Grammar'. When the youth had finished his education, he was engaged to Mr Heath as an engraver – but left it off, and wholly devoted his time to making designs and drawing them on the wood, for the wood engravers.

† Henry Fulke Woolcomb Plantagenet Hole, left Newcastle and went thence to Liverpool where he was patronized by Mr Roscoe, Capel Loft, Maccreery the printer and others; he continued in Liverpool untill the death of his grandfather — Hole Esqre of Ebberly Hall, Devonshire to whose very large property he fell heir to, and left off pursuing the arts any longer.

[185]

nephew John Harrison, was chiefly employed on writing engraving – he died of epileptic fits and was buried at North Shields church, between two trees near the foot path. Henry White, from London, was engaged to me to serve out the remainder of his apprenticeship, when his master, the late Mr Lee died. When the term of his engagement with me was ended, he returned to London, and chiefly turned his attention to the imitation of sketchy *cross hatching* on wood, from the inimitable pencil of Mr Cruikshank, and perhaps some other artists in this same way. Henry White appears to have taken the lead of others, who followed that manner of cutting, which shortly became *quite the Ton*. Another of my pupils of distinguished ability, both as a draftsman and wood engraver, was Luke Clennell whose melencholly history, will be well remembered by the artists of London and else where, and the simpathetic feelings which was drawn forth and shewn to him by a generous public, by their subscriptions to a print of the battle of Waterloo, from his painting of the decisive charge of the Guards, on that eventfull day. The next of my pupils was Isaac Nicholson, who was both a good apprentice and a good artist. His engravings on wood are clearly, or honestly cut, as well as being accurately done from his patterns; he did not pursue his business in London, but carries it on in Newcastle. The next of my pupils, and one of the first in excellence was William Harvey, who both as an engraver and designer, stands preeminent at this day. His fellow apprentice was William Temple (who left off wood engraving, and commenced linnen draper in Newcastle), he was a faithfull copyest, and his pieces were honestly or clearly cut. The last apprentice I had was John Armstrong, who is now pursuing his business in London. I have not gone down in regular succession with my pupils, but I have noticed all those who (in my estimation) were worth notice and now when the time is fast approaching for my winding up all my labours, I may be allowed to name my own son and partner, whose time has been taken up with attending to all the branches of our business and who I trust will not let wood engraving go down, and tho he has not shewn any partiallity towards it – yet the talent is there, if he will and I hope call it forth.

[186]

21

How far I may venture further to obtrude my opinions or advice on the notice of artists, particularly to engravers on wood, I know not, but they may readily imagine that I cannot help feeling a deep interest, and an ardent desire, that the art may long flourish, and that those who follow it may feel happy in the pursuit. Perhaps, what I have already said, may be thought not uninteresting to some of them, and if I knew how I could go further in any way that might urge or stimulate them to feel an enthusiasm for this art, it should not be awanting; for this wish, 'tho tottering on the downhill of life, is extended bejond the grave.

The sedentary artist ought if possible to have his dwelling in the country, where he could follow his business undisturbed, surrounded by pleasing rural scenery and the fresh air, and as 'all work and no play, makes Jack a dull boy', he ought not to sit at it too long at a time, but to unbend his mind with some variety of employment – for which purpose it is desireable that artists, with their *little cots*, should also have each a garden attached, in which they might find both exercise and amusement – and only occasionally visit the city or the smokey town, and that chiefly for the purpose of meetings with their brother artists in which they might make an interchange of their sentiments and commune with each other as to whatever regarded the arts. And were I allowed to become their M.D., my prescription shall cost them nothing and be *easily taken* – it being only attentively to observe two or three rules. The first of which is, that they will contrive to be very hungry once a day – never send a second supply to the stomach, till the first has left it, and never to indulge to satietey in eating any thing. By persisting in this, they would find their reward in great good health and a vigorous unclouded mind; and [by] a little observation, they may clearly see that a great portion of mankind live to eat, not eat to live. To say more to men of sense and artists – which a desire to contribute everything in my power towards their peace of mind and happiness prompts me to do – I may be allowed to add, that those of them who have attained to eminence will find themselves pursued by envy; for 'There is no species of hatred greater than that which a man of mediocrity bears to a man of genius; his reach of thought, his successful combinations, and his sudden felicities are never forgiven by those whom nature has fashioned in a less perfect mould.' It is the duty of parents and guardians of youth to endeavour with the utmost care to discover their capacities and their

[187]

fitness for pursuing any business, before they are engaged in it, but particularly for such as are intended to be put to learn the fine arts for without they are innately gifted with the power for becoming artists, the want of it will be found to be to them *uphill-work* and be productive of unhappiness to them 'thro life; but the fondness of parents for their offspring is mostly such as to make them so blind as to think them fit to learn any thing and disappointment follows them like a shadow. It would be well, for such parents to read Gay's fable of 'The Owl, the Swan, the Cock, the Spider, the Ass and the Farmer' [and the] Dodsley fable of 'The Eagle and the Owl'. It may indeed be conceeded that there are some rare exceptions to this general rule, for a man may be so formed in body and mind – with such cimitry and health in the one, and such energy in the other – that they may attain a great way towards perfection, in any thing they ardently pursue, but an 'Admirable Crichton', and a Sir Joshua Reynolds do not appear every day. Men so gifted by nature, whether as artists or in any other way where intellectual powers are to be drawn forth, ought never to despair of rising to eminence, for it is wrong in them to take it into their heads that they can never equal such men *of this character*, as have excelled all others in their day; but they ought to keep in mind that the same superintending providence, which gifted these men with talents to excite wonder and to improve society from time to time in all ages, still rules the world and the affairs of mankind, and will continue to do the same for ever – as often as the services of such men are wanted. And this consideration ought to act as a stimulant to their successors, to endeavour to surpass in excellence the brilliant luminaries who have only gone before them to pave the way and to enlighten their paths. Had I been a painter, I never would have copied the works of '*Old Masters*' or others, however highly they might be esteemed. I would have gone to nature for *all my patterns*, for she exhibits an endless variety – not possible to be surpassed and scarcely ever to be equalled. I would indeed have endeavoured to find out the way how these artists of old made or compounded their excellent colours, as well as the disposition of their lights and shades by which they were enabled to accomplish so much and so well. All artists (and indeed all men) ought when necessary to divide their time, by regularly appropriating one portion of it to one purpose, and another part of it to the varied business that may be set apart for another. In this way a deal of work may be easily got through and the artist (after leaving off his too intense application) would see, as it were, what he had been doing with *new eyes* – by which he would be enabled to criticise the almost endless variety of lights, shades and effects etc which awaits his pencil to

[188]

produce. But the work of the painter may be said to be as endless as the objects which nature continually presents to his view, and it is his judgement that must direct him in the choice of such as may be interesting, or otherwise; in this he will see what others have done before him, and the shoals and quicksands that have retarded their progress as well as the rocks they have at last entirely split upon. On his taking a proper survey of all this, he will see the *labour-in-vain* that has been bestowed upon useless designs, which have and will continue to find their way to a garret; while those well chosen and well executed subjects, will, from their excellence be preserved, with perhaps increasing value for ages to come. In performing all this, great industry will perhaps be required and it ought ever to be kept in mind, that as in morals nothing is worth listning to but truth – so in arts nothing is worth looking at but such productions as have been faithfully copied from nature; but poetry indeed may launch out [and] take further liberties to charm the intellectual minds of its votaries. It is only such youths as providence has gifted with strong, intellectual, innate powers, that are perfectly fit to embark in the fine arts – and the power and propensity to do so, is often seen early to bud out and shew itself in the various ways which youth is destined to pursue. This is first seen in the young musician, who without having even learned his ABCs breaks out with a random kind of unrestrained freedom to whistle and sing, and how often have I been amused at the first assays of the plowboy, and how charmed to find him so soon attempt to equal his whistling and singing master at the plow-stilts, and who with avidity uneasing – never stopped 'till he thought he excelled him. The *future painter* is shewn by his strong propensity to sketch out whatever objects in nature attract his attention, and excites him to imitate them. The poet indeed has more difficulties to contend with at first, than the others, because he must know language, or be furnished with words wherewith to enable him to express himself even in his first assays, in his dogerel metre and *singsong rhymes*. In all the varied ways by which naturalists and artists are befitted to enlighten, to charm and to embellish civilized society, as they advance through life – if they entertain the true feeling that every production they behold is created not by chance, but by design – [they] will find an encreasing and endless pleasure in the exhaustless stores which *nature has provided*, to attract the attention and promote the happiness of her votaries during the term of their sojourning here. The painter nead not roam very far from his home in any part of our beautifull isles, to meet with plenty of charming scenes from which to copy nature – either in an extended or limited scale – and in which he may give full scope to his genious and to his pencil, either in animate or inanimate subjects. Whether he searches for such in the narrowed romantic ravine – the placid holme – the hollow dell, or the pendant foliage of the richly ornamented dean with the burns which have, by time, been scooped out and which roar or dash through their bottoms, or run murmuring from pool to pool through their pebbly beds – all these bounded and bordered with a back ground of ivey covered ancient hollow oaks, with elms, willow and birch (thus clothed, as if to hide their age – or kindly to offer shelter to an undergrowth of hazel, whins, broom, juniper and heather with the wild rose and woodbine and brambles – beset with clumps of fern and foxglove) – while the edges of the mossy braes are covered with a profusion of wild flowers, which 'blow to blush unseen' or which peep out among the creeping ground-lings – the bleaberry, wild strawberry, harebell, violet and such like; but I feel a want of words to enable the pen to give an adequate description of the beauty and simplicity of these neglected spots, which dame nature has planted as if to invite the admiration of such as have hearts and eyes befitted to appreciate and enjoy these her exquisite treats, while she may perhaps smile at the formal pruning efforts of the gardner as well as doubt whether the pencil of the artist will ever accomplish a correct imitation. But be all this as it may, she has spread out her beauties to feast the eyes and to invite the admiration of all mankind, and to whet them up to an ardent love of all her works. How often have I, in my angling excursions, loitered upon the such sunny braes, lost in extacy, and wishing I could impart to others the pleasures I felt upon such occasions – but they must see with their own eyes to feel as I felt, and form their own opinion how far the scenes depictured by poets come up to or fall short [of the reality]. The naturalist's poet, Thomson, has done as much as he could; so have others. Allan Ramsay's 'Habbies Howe' where 'a' thy sweets of spring and summer grow' may have been covered with beauties such as I have noticed – but the man smit with a fit turn of mind and inclined to search out for such *beauty spots* will not nead the aids of poets to help him in his enthusiastic ardour.

GLOSSARY

balls, the wooden-handled leather pads used for applying ink before the invention of the inking roller in the early 19th century.

beild, shelter or refuge.

boat stower, boat hook or punt pole.

brea, hill.

chare, narrow lane or alley.

click-hook, large salmon hooks bound together shaft to shaft. Poachers used them to strike fish in the belly. Click: to snatch, seize, steal (Northumberland).

cree, soften.

dreg, bar of iron put between spokes of a wheel to act as a brake.

dyking mitten, glove for wall building.

a fac, a small block displaying an initial letter and a view of Newcastle and St Nicholas's church lantern spire.

fitters, coal-brokers who sold and loaded coals.

flaid, frightened.

flipes, hat brim.

fother, cartload.

gallow pots, small earthenware pots, possibly with handles for hanging.

galloway, a pony, small saddle horse of a strong breed formerly peculiar to Galloway in south-west Scotland.

garth, small piece of enclosed ground near the home, paddock.

gills, ravines, narrow valleys or wooden glens with streams.

gin, gin driver, the colliery gin was a rope-winding device to which horses were harnessed, situated at the head of pit shafts for raising the coal.

glead, the common kite.

gorfoot, the carrion crow.

guiseing, masquerade, dressed for a mumming.

haugh, level ground by riverside.

Hedley Kow, the name of a 'bogle' or sprite connected with the Northumberland village of Hedley.

hirpling, limping.

hoppings, country wakes, annual festivals in Northumberland.

jackleg knife, pocket knife, large clasp knife with single, broad, square-edged blade. Possibly derived from the name of the cutler inventor, Jacques de Liège.

kirn supper, harvest home, supper held on completion of harvest.
kylo, small breed of Highland cattle.

lave, to bale or draw water.
leish, well-made, lithe.
lonnings, lanes or by-roads.
lown, sheltered side.

mall, hammer.
messet dog, pet or lap dog.
muck the byer, to clean out the cowshed or stable.

nice, exact.

pinfold, enclosure for strayed cattle.
pought nets, nets fastened to poles with which fishermen poked the river banks to force out the fish.

saughs, sallow or willow.
'*seddle boards*', the boards or frame work at the top of a coal pit.
set gads, stakes for fixing a fishing set or fixed net; or standing fishing rods. See Bewick's tail-piece on p.169.
shive, slice.
silkey, (Northumberland) supernatural being popularly called silkey from the nature of her robes. See James Hardy, 'Silky: A Northumbrian Tradition', *Alnwick Mercury*, 1 March 1862.
sinker, digger of mine shafts.
a Sir Walter Blackett, a political turncoat.
smout hole, smout, the fry of salmon.
sods, rough saddle made of coarse cloth or skin, stuffed with straw.
strike, possibly boards or timbers set in the river bed to divert a deep water flow at a ford; or simply a fishermen's station.
sykes, ditches.

whins, common furze bushes.